"Every volunteer encounter Carol Lee Hall dedicates her original ... encouraging those of us who have at times felt passion ... weariness or frustration. So turn to the side, pick up this devotional, and let the Lord refresh your spirit."

Pastor Kevin Hom, young singles and young families pastor,
Fremont Community Church, Fremont, CA

"*For Those Who Serve* is a series of practical examples of people in ministry. Each one faces the kind of problems we have all experienced. Supported by Scripture texts and study passages, Carol Hall's stories present clever portrayals of realistic people. She shares penetrating insights with touches of unexpected humor. The reader will find here dozens of ways to face the challenges of ministry in partnership with the God who has gifted and called us all to serve."

Ethel Herr, author and speaker

"These devotional stories accompanied by applicable Scriptures will assist, encourage, and affirm church volunteers. The straightforward presentation of the importance of commitment, faithfulness, setting priorities, using gifts, and leadership growth will provide help and hope for situations involving discouragement and burnout. Blessings will multiply as you are helped to face the challenges of a volunteer ministry."

Barbara Bolton, author and speaker

"*For Those Who Serve* offers basic advice to those with a heart to serve God. The author has created a collection of true-to-life vignettes depicting problems that arise particularly in areas of church ministry. She skillfully guides the reader to practical solutions based on an understanding of God's Word. A bonus gained by reading this book is the insight one gets into the heart of a well-organized church that is harnessing the skills and labor of its volunteers."

Mrs. John Phillips

"This devotional will encourage, challenge, motivate, and recharge those who serve the Lord in the local church. The well-chosen Scriptures and the "too-true" stories will resonate with real-life experiences volunteers face doing God's work. I highly recommend *For Those Who Serve* for the volunteer and those who equip volunteers."

Steve Quen, pastor, Bay Area Chinese Bible Church

1) Amplify your praise

2) Experience the pleasure of God - praise prophetic act of faith

3) Identify your greatest strength God + honor your great talents in G

4) Engage heaven in a brand new way in favor

5) Use your gifts for His Highest & best & serve others Go & exalt you to highest pla

6) Search for meaning & significance finds fulfillment + satisfaction

In season of Hope deferred + needed release

For Those Who Serve

A Devotional for Church Volunteers

Carol Lee Hall

Baker Books

A Division of Baker Book House Co
Grand Rapids, Michigan 49516

Published by Baker Books
a division of Baker Book House Company
P.O. Box 6287, Grand Rapids, MI 49516-6287
www.bakerbooks.com

Printed in the United States of America

Library of Congress Cataloging-in-Publication Data
Hall, Carol Lee, 1959–
    For those who serve : a devotional for church volunteers / Carol Lee Hall.
        p.   cm.
    Includes index.
    ISBN 0-8010-6462-7 (pbk.)
    1. Volunteers—Prayer-books and devotions—English. I. Title.
BV283.V64H35 2004
242′.69—dc22   2003019621

To my husband, Ed, and daughter, Jennifer

Contents

Acknowledgments

I would like to thank these people who helped make this book possible:

Ethel Herr, whom I consider my writing mentor and friend, for her inspiration and advice;

Vicki Crumpton, for championing my work at Baker Books;

Margaret Chan, David and Greta Chew, Sherry Corley, Cyndi Lee, Stacey Lee, Debbie Leong, Gloria Ong, Annette Siu, CJ Tam, Julie Wong, and Ginger Yee for their topic suggestions and other input;

John Vonhof, Mary Watkins, and the other members of our writers group for their critiques;

Karen Leong and the Friday Ladies Bible Study for their prayers and encouragement;

Knight and Jimmy of Leong Photography;

Pastor Steve Quen, for his thoughtful advice and assurance;

Ed Hall, my husband, whose emotional, spiritual, and financial support enabled me to pursue my dream of writing;

Jennifer Hall, my daughter, for her smiles and laughter at the end of my writing day;

Marion Lee, my mother, who always believed I could do anything I set my mind to.

Preface

The volunteer situations and characters depicted in this book are fictional. Some stories and characters are inspired by real events, people, or a combination of people, but the details and names have been changed. Others are purely made up. My hope is that readers will see themselves in the characters and relate to their circumstances and feelings. A variety of church ministries and community situations are depicted. Of course, no one church or city will include them all, but my desire is that the lessons in the stories will be applicable to many different areas.

Each devotion includes a short Bible reading, bonus Bible reference for those who wish to delve deeper into the topic, story, application, and prayer. Some devotions are tied in to related Bible stories that are mentioned in one of the two references. The applications deal with heart matters and practical ministry ideas for volunteers and church leaders, paid or not. My aim is to encourage Christians to serve God cheerfully and effectively, motivated and empowered by the Holy Spirit.

Steady As She Goes

Let us fix our eyes on Jesus, the author and perfecter of our faith.

Hebrews 12:2

Bonus Reading: Hebrews 12:1–3

"Are you *sure* you want to go on *that* ride?" I asked my group on the school field trip.

"Yes, yes! It looks like so much fun!" my daughter and her two friends answered.

I looked up at the rockets orbiting a planet. As they flew round and round, connected to the globe by only a thin metal bar, my stomach started turning. Glancing at my watch, I noticed it was almost time for everyone to return to the school bus. *If I get sick, at least my whole day won't be ruined.*

"All right," I sighed. "I'll have to ride with you because you're not tall enough to go by yourselves. Then we *must* leave."

We got in line for our last ride at the amusement park. I noticed each rocket had its own control for moving up and down as it followed the others around the planet.

Please, God, don't let me feel nauseous after this ride, I prayed as we boarded our rocket.

I had been prone to motion sickness since I was a child. As we settled ourselves securely in the rocket, I remembered what my mother always told me during long automobile rides: "Look straight ahead. Don't look to the side at the cars or scenery passing by."

The rockets blasted off and soon we were cruising around the planet, each at a different height off terra firma. I focused my eyes on the rocket directly in front of me, but the make-believe spacemen inside took great pleasure in jerking their rocket up and down repeatedly in rapid succession. My stomach began to churn. I switched my eyes to the next rocket, whose astronauts controlled their ship on a steady course around the middle of the planet.

Meanwhile, my little spacegirls took turns flying their rocket all the way up and all the way down in gradual sweeping motions. I kept my eyes focused on the steady ship in front of me. It seemed to stay perfectly still as the rest of the amusement park whirled by.

At the end of the ride, all the rockets touched down to earth. The girls hopped out easily as I slowly rose, grasping the edge of the rocket to steady myself. Surprisingly, I felt neither dizzy nor sick! I breathed a prayer of thanksgiving to the Lord.

"Let's go, girls!" I called as they tried to get back in line.

Sometimes life takes us on a ride we don't like, and our problems and activities whirl around so fast that we get queasy thinking about them. But if we keep our eyes on Jesus, the steady and unchanging One, he will take us through and give us power to sort through our problems and prioritize our activities to provide a sense of order, peace, and equilibrium in our lives.

Immutable God, help me to always put you first in my life and keep me from getting overwhelmed by my problems. Show me what is important and give me the "peace which transcends all understanding." I let you order my life.

I've Got Confidence

Put no confidence in the flesh.

Philippians 3:3

Bonus Reading: Philippians 3:3–11

Brad volunteered on the church audiovisual crew. Ever since grade school, he had been interested in electronics, gadgets, and computers. A hardware engineer by profession, he fit AV perfectly. When the church needed to buy new equipment, Milt, the head of AV, always consulted Brad, the "electronics whiz." Whenever the equipment malfunctioned, Brad handled it effortlessly—until one fateful Sunday when the soundboard blew out.

Right in the middle of Pastor Jim's sermon there was a loud "boom" and then silence. The congregation saw the pastor's mouth moving, but heard nothing. Five hundred people began murmuring and turning their heads back and up toward the sound booth. It looked empty! After what seemed like an eternity, Brad's head popped up, his face sweaty but controlled as he attempted to hide the panic in his heart.

Think, Brad, think. No smoke. Good. No fire. Check the wires. Fine. The switches. Okay. The connections. Great. The wireless mike. The usher's bringing it back here. Looks good to me. What was I doing just before it blew? Nothing out of the ordinary. I don't know what else to do. God, I can find nothing wrong with the equipment. Please make it work.

Brad pressed the "on" button. Nothing.

Pastor Jim cleared his throat and shouted, "I guess I'll have to finish the sermon without a mike."

The service continued without incident, although Pastor Jim asked for water twice. After the last "amen," Milt walked up to Brad outside the booth. "What happened in there today?"

Brad related all the steps he took. Milt assured him, "It seems like you went through all the correct procedures."

"I guess God was just reminding me that I have to rely on him and not on myself or my own knowledge," Brad said.

"Let's check this out together and ask God for his wisdom," Milt said as the two headed inside the booth.

We may be very gifted in our volunteer areas, but we must never rely on our talents alone. In Philippians, Paul writes that out of all the Jews, he could be considered the most "Jewish" and could have relied on his own righteousness for salvation, but instead he chose to rely on Christ alone.

Gracious heavenly Father, you have given me many talents, but I can do nothing without you. Enable me to use my abilities for you, not with self-confidence, but with God-confidence that you will bring glory to your name through them.

Dial Tone

So in everything, do to others what you would have them do to you,
for this sums up the Law and the Prophets.

Matthew 7:12

Bonus Reading: Matthew 22:37–40

"Hello, my name is Bill and I'm calling on behalf of the Midtown Newspaper . . ."

"We don't want it and I wish you'd stop calling. GOOD-BYE!" Lucinda slammed down the kitchen phone. "Why do they always call when I'm in the middle of writing the church bulletin?" she complained aloud.

Resuming her seat at the family computer, Lucinda put the finishing touches on the bulletin and e-mailed it to the church secretary. After lunch, she scanned her list of other volunteer duties. She picked up the phone to begin calling new visitors from the previous Sunday.

"Hello, Mrs. Wright? My name is Lucinda Armstrong and I'm calling from Grace Community Church . . ."

"Again? Two other people called this week from your church. I already told them our family was just visiting one time and not planning to come back. Now I really know I'm not coming back. GOOD-BYE!"

"She sure is rude!" Lucinda remarked. Then it struck her. *I treated the telephone salesman the same way.*

Confessing her sin, she finished her calls. Later that evening while she was making dinner, the telephone rang.

"Good evening, my name is Heather and I'd like to tell you about a special offer your credit card company has for you . . ."

"I appreciate the call, Heather, but we're not interested. Please try someone else. Thank you anyway. Good-bye."

"But this offer is unlike any we've had before, and it will save you a great deal of money."

Lucinda repeated herself word for word, emphasizing the word "not," and finally hung up the phone, feeling satisfied with the way she handled the call.

The Golden Rule, as Matthew 7:12 is known, applies as much today as it did in Bible times. Lucinda realized that salespeople are only doing their jobs, however annoying their calls are, especially when she is busy.

Dear God, thank you for never hanging up on me. Help me to always remember my Christian testimony, even when talking to strangers on the phone. If I'm not interested in what they have to offer, give me wisdom to graciously, yet quickly, end the conversation.

A Child's Faith

Elisha said, "Go around and ask all your neighbors for empty jars. Don't ask for just a few." . . . When all the jars were full, she said to her son, "Bring me another one." But he replied, "There is not a jar left." Then the oil stopped flowing.

2 Kings 4:3, 6

Bonus Reading: 2 Kings 4:1–7

"Why are we getting all these empty boxes, Dad?" six-year-old Keifer asked.

Myron balanced the produce boxes on top of a shopping cart. "We're going to put blankets, soap, and food in them for homeless people," he replied.

"Right now?"

"No, we're going to drive these boxes down to the church and store them there." The double doors of the supermarket automatically opened as Myron carefully maneuvered the cart out to his minivan.

"Where are we going to get the blankets and stuff to put in the boxes?" Keifer asked as he helped his dad pile them into the van.

"People from the church are going to donate them. We already have some items stored in the shed behind the church. This Sunday is the last day for people to bring things in. Then you and I and several folks are going to put everything in the boxes and take them down to the mission on First Street." Myron loaded the last box and shut the car door.

When his dad slid into the driver's seat, Keifer said, "I looked in that shed last Sunday. There wasn't much in there. Dad, I think we have too many boxes."

"People always wait until the last minute. But we have to pray that God will remind everyone to bring something for the homeless this Sunday. By having the boxes ready, we're going to be prepared for however God blesses." Myron started the van and backed out of the parking space.

"It's kinda like the lesson we had in Sunday school a couple of weeks ago. Elisha told a lady and her sons to borrow a whole buncha jars from their neighbors. She had just a little bit of oil, but Elisha told her to keep pouring it into the jars until it ran out. She had just enough for all the jars. Dad, do you think God will bless us like that?"

Myron chuckled. "Anything is possible with God. We have to have faith that the Lord will bless our efforts. But if we have a couple of boxes left over, that's okay too."

They drove toward the church in silence for a moment. Suddenly Keifer asked, "Dad, after we drop off these boxes, can we go to another supermarket and get some more?"

In childlike faith, Keifer believed the more boxes they got, the more God would bless. In the story of the widow's oil, that family's faith in God was exhibited by how many empty jars they collected. God's provision is only limited by our faith and obedience to him.

Great Provider, sometimes I have trouble believing that you will bless my efforts on your behalf. I take heart in the story of the widow's oil and pray that I will not limit your blessings on my life. I know that you are capable of doing more than I would ever imagine or ask.

It's Not Your Fault

Who can discern his errors?
  Forgive my hidden faults.
Keep your servant also from willful sins;
  may they not rule over me.
Then will I be blameless,
  innocent of great transgression.

Psalm 19:12–13

Bonus Reading: Philippians 3:13–14

"Hi, this is Hoshi. I'm sorry, but we have to cancel class again today. My son has a fever and I have to stay home to take care of him. Please do me a favor and call Edna. Thanks so much."

Hoshi hung up the phone. She and an assistant had started the ladies exercise class two years ago for the seniors in her church. This year her helper found a full-time job and had to quit. Hoshi felt strongly that God was leading her to continue the class alone. However, her three children seemed to be taking turns getting sick. She picked up the receiver and punched in another number.

"Blanche? Hoshi. My son is ill and we have to call off the session today. I'm so sorry."

"Again? This is the third time this year! Why don't you get another assistant to take over for you? Are you dressing your kids warmly enough? I have a recipe for chicken soup that will chase any cold away . . ." Blanche went on and on.

After ten minutes, Hoshi hung up and put her head in her arms. She cried, "Lord, I know it's not my fault the kids keep getting sick. But I feel so guilty for letting the ladies down. I feel like I'm disappointing you too. Do you really want me to continue?"

After drying her tears, Hoshi picked up the phone again. "Hi Vera, this is Hoshi. I'm sorry, but we have to cancel class today. Seiji is sick."

"Don't feel sorry; we understand. I was thinking, whenever you can't make it, the ladies could just go walking instead. It won't be the same kind of exercise you do with us, but at least we'll be moving around. I'll tell everyone when they get there you can't make it and whoever wants to go walking can stay."

"That's a great idea, Vera! Thank you for thinking of it. But three ladies have already been told class is called off."

"No problem, tell me who they are and I'll give them a ring."

After supplying Vera with the names and phone numbers, Hoshi hung up feeling much better.

Some Christians feel guilty about past sins, letting people down, or situations out of their control. This emotion can be crippling if left to fester and grow. God has forgiven and forgotten all our sins. He is in control of every situation. He doesn't hold us accountable for other people's actions.

Faithful Forgiver, I am so afraid of disappointing people. I always wonder if I should have done more. Please free me of unnecessary feelings of guilt.

Bacon and Eggs

If anyone would come after me, he must deny himself and take up his cross and follow me.

Matthew 16:24

Bonus Reading: Matthew 16:24–28

"Let's start with the picnic tables and throw all trash into the garbage cans," the picnic clean-up director said.

Henry and Dean, identical twins, picked up half-empty cups of soda and plates of chicken bones and corncobs and threw them into the waste can. Then they started at one end of a table and rolled up the paper tablecloth, enclosing the remaining trash inside.

"Two hundred people can sure make a mess," Henry commented. The young men lifted the bundle into the can and started on the next table.

"When the cans are full, take out the plastic bags, tie them, and throw them into the dumpster at the back of the church," the director instructed as he pointed to the huge green container at the far end of the grassy picnic area. "I'll take care of the barbeque pits."

The twins piled the bags at the edge of the farthest table, ready to bring all of them over in as few trips as possible. After they cleared the final table, they plopped down on the picnic bench. Dean wiped sweat off his forehead with his arm. In a few seconds, Henry jumped up. "Come on, Dean, let's bring these over to the dumpster."

"You go ahead. I want to sit here another minute," Dean replied.

Henry shrugged and picked up four bags. On his way back, he saw Dean slowly rise, pick up one bag, and head toward him.

"What's the matter with your other hand? Your eighteenth birthday got you down?" Henry teased.

"This is heavy," Dean whined.

When they finished throwing in the last bag, Henry said, "Let's check the bathrooms. Those cans are probably overflowing."

Dean screwed up his face. "I'm not going in there. The director didn't tell us to."

"But it needs to be done anyway. Think of what it's going to look like tomorrow morning when visitors come to church. Are you coming or not?"

Dean shook his head. "I did my duty. Catch a ride home with someone else, okay?"

"Suit yourself," Henry shrugged as he headed for the bathrooms.

Henry enthusiastically went the extra mile, but Dean whined and did the least he could get away with. Henry stayed until the job was done, but Dean left after dumping a few garbage bags. Henry viewed his volunteering as service for God, but Dean saw it as an obligation to his church.

Someone once said the difference between involvement and dedication is like the difference between bacon and eggs. The chicken was involved in producing the egg, but the pig dedicated his life to provide us with bacon.

Precious Lord, I'm involved in church, but I sense that you want me to raise my level of commitment. Help me to stick with it when the going gets tough and I feel like quitting. I am willing to give my all for you.

Please Stay

And the things you have heard me say in the presence of many witnesses entrust to reliable men who will also be qualified to teach others.

2 Timothy 2:2

Bonus Reading: Psalm 37:3–6

Priscilla loved to sew. Since the age of fifteen, she had been making her own clothes, gifts, and home decor items. When she heard the church needed people to sew costumes for the Easter play, she jumped at the chance. The church began to know her as "the sewing lady." Other women interested in sewing came to her for advice. They formed their own sewing circle. The church began to count on them to make various items for the church, ranging from Christmas banners to blankets for the homeless. Their ministry grew by leaps and bounds, mainly due to Priscilla's leadership and knack for retaining committed volunteers.

"What's your secret?" Dolores asked Priscilla one day after services.

"What do you mean?"

"How do you keep all those women in the sewing circle? I mean, I like sewing, but I don't think I could do it as much as those women do. Why do they keep coming?"

"Well, we care about each other," Priscilla began. "When we get together, we don't just sew, we talk. We talk about what concerns us in our lives at the time. We help each other and give each other ideas. We are there for one another."

"It almost sounds like you have a small group home team," Dolores commented.

"In a way, it is. It hasn't always had smooth sailing, though. At one point, we almost lost half our women," Priscilla said.

"What happened?"

"Someone complained that we were given too much work and that they couldn't handle it. All of a sudden, several women said they wanted to leave the group. I promised I would talk to the church leadership and tell them we couldn't accommodate all the projects people wanted us to do. I also provided resources for the ones with less experience so they wouldn't feel lost. It was scary for awhile."

We must do everything we can to encourage committed volunteers. The first step is to build their trust. We can do that by being available to help them and listen when they have a problem. We need to pray for them and provide resources to make their job easier.

True One, please raise up committed volunteers to assist in my ministry. Help me to encourage them in the work and do my part to keep them interested.

I Can't Forgive Myself

For I will forgive their wickedness
and will remember their sins no more.

Hebrews 8:12

Bonus Reading: Romans 4:6–8

Lotus sat dejectedly in front of her bathroom mirror. *Why was I so stupid? Why couldn't I have just held my tongue and waited until we were leaving?*

Lotus thought back to the previous day's events. It was Secretary's Day and the regular office staff had gone out to lunch with the pastor. Since she and Charity had days off, they volunteered to fill in for a couple of hours.

Lotus sorted mail while Charity photocopied minutes from the last business meeting. Lotus was dying to find out if a rumor she had heard was true.

After an hour and a half, she finally blurted out, "I heard Ari broke up with you. Is that true?"

Charity dropped a ream of paper she was trying to reload into the machine. The sheets scattered onto the floor. Lotus bent down to help Charity retrieve the paper. Lotus noticed blood dripping from her friend's finger.

"You have a paper cut. Let me get you a tissue." She grabbed a tissue from the box on the desk and handed it to Charity. "I'm sorry if my question caught you off guard. You don't have to answer it."

Charity sighed. "I guess everybody knows by now. It's just . . ." She began to cry.

Stupid me, stupid me, Lotus kept saying to herself as she tried to comfort Charity. *Look how I've made her feel. Oh no, the secretaries are back early. Charity will be embarrassed to have everyone see her crying. If only I'd kept my big mouth shut . . .*

Lotus took Charity to the rest room where Charity had a good cry. Afterwards, Charity said, "I needed to let it all out. Don't feel bad for bringing it up."

Lotus managed a weak smile. "I hope you feel better."

Lotus kept berating herself for making Charity cry. Even though Charity forgave her, Lotus couldn't forgive herself. When God forgives us of our sins, he forgets them too. We don't have to carry around a load of guilt—he has freed us.

Forgiver of sins, I can't let myself off the hook. I know in my head you have pardoned me, but I can't seem to shake guilty thoughts. It is comforting to know you don't keep records of my faults. Free me from this mental net.

I Need a Vacation!

> When the apostles returned, they reported to Jesus what they had done. Then he took them with him and they withdrew by themselves to a town called Bethsaida.
>
> Luke 9:10

Bonus Reading: Mark 6:30–32

Terrill had barely sat down in a back pew when the church treasurer tapped him on the shoulder. "Elder Terrill? Can you sign these check request forms? The bills need to be paid this week." Terrill took out his pen as the congregation sang a hymn. He quickly signed his name on each paper and handed them back to the treasurer.

Terrill opened his bulletin and scanned the meetings for this week. He shook his head. Sunday school teachers right after service, Missions Committee on Wednesday night. Before the next song, someone else tapped him on the back. Terrill turned to see the mens ensemble leader holding a stack of sheet music. "These are for the singing engagement in two months. First practice is this Thursday night." Terrill smiled weakly as he took the papers.

During the message, Terrill began to nod off. His wife jabbed him in the side. He sat up with a start. The parishioners in front of him turned their heads. From the corner of his eye he saw his wife glaring at him. Terrill struggled to stay awake for the rest of the sermon.

Needless to say, Terrill's church responsibilities burnt him out. When he shared his problem with his pastor, Terrill heard a surprising answer. "Take a vacation from church!" the pastor suggested. "Go visit another church next week."

"But Pastor, what will people think of me?" Terrill asked.

"Don't worry about other people," the pastor said. He leaned closer and whispered, "Where do you think preachers go on Sundays when they're on vacation but don't leave town?"

Terrill laughed. "I see your point. If you came here, you wouldn't get any rest."

The next week, Terrill and his family visited a church across town. The usher offered a friendly greeting to the "new ones." He ushered them to a front pew where Terrill enjoyed the worship time. He concentrated on the minister's message without interruption. When the service was over, he felt refreshed, revitalized, and ready to serve God back at his home church.

Are you burnt out from your church responsibilities? Perhaps you need to withdraw yourself for a time of rest and reflection on God. Visit a church of like faith to recharge your batteries. Then come back ready to enjoy your service for God at your home church.

Restorer of my soul, I need a vacation! Renew my spirit so I can serve you with a better attitude and replenished vigor. May I take the time to rest and worship you.

Stand Graciously

Please test your servants for ten days: Give us nothing but vegetables to eat and water to drink. Then compare our appearance with that of the young men who eat the royal food, and treat your servants in accordance with what you see.

Daniel 1:12–13

Bonus Reading: Daniel 1:8–20

Midori held the ladder while Nadia stapled a placard onto a telephone pole. "Martin for City Council" topped four other signs touting various city council candidates. After Nadia descended, Midori folded up the ladder and began walking over to the next pole. She turned around and noticed Nadia picking at the lowest placard.

"What are you doing, Nadia?"

Nadia threw something onto the ground. "Just loosening some of these staples."

Midori came back and whispered, "But then the sign will fall down."

"You get the picture."

Midori put the ladder down and said in a low voice, "But that's not fair to him."

"Fair, schmair. They do it to ours. Everybody does it," Nadia said as the sign drooped to one side. "Let's get out of here before it actually drops." Nadia quickly scooped up a pile of "Martin" signs from the sidewalk, and the two walked over to the next pole.

Midori pursed her lips. As they arrived at the sign-clad pole, she said, "This time you hold the ladder and I'll put up the sign." As Midori reached the second rung, she said, "Hand me the staple gun."

Nadia reached into her pocket and fished out the gun. After stapling the sign, Midori stepped down. When Nadia moved the ladder to one side, Midori edged over and planted herself directly in front of the pole, effectively blocking Nadia's access to the signs. "We're done," she said quickly. "Let's go back to the truck now."

Nadia shrugged her shoulders and picked up the ladder. The truck was parked close to the first pole. The two women put the ladder and extra signs in the back of the pickup truck. Midori planned to come back later without Nadia and restaple the crooked sign, but as she opened the passenger door, Nadia asked for the staple gun.

Midori reluctantly handed her the tool, and Nadia returned to the first pole and restapled the opponent's sign. When Midori gave her a perplexed look, Nadia said simply, "You got to me."

Midori could have reacted to Nadia's indiscretion in a holier-than-thou way—spouting Scripture, lecturing, or stapling the sign back on right in front of Nadia. Instead, she spoke quietly and also let her actions do the talking. In the Bible, Daniel and his three friends did not rebel against the king's official but negotiated with the guard to try an experiment. Daniel's practical and creative solution saved their lives without compromising their convictions. We need to stand for our beliefs, but choose our words and actions carefully.

Dear God, give me courage to take a stand for you. Show me when to speak and when to be quiet. May my actions back up my words.

Finding Child Care

I [Nehemiah] also said to him, "If it pleases the king, may I have letters to the governors of Trans-Euphrates, so that they will provide me safe-conduct until I arrive in Judah? And may I have a letter to Asaph, keeper of the king's forest, so he will give me timber to make beams for the gates of the citadel by the temple and for the city wall and for the residence I will occupy?" And because the gracious hand of my God was upon me, the king granted my requests.

Nehemiah 2:7–8

Bonus Reading: Numbers 32:16–19

Jeannette's three small children scrambled over her as she sat on the couch with the phone. "I do want to come back for hospital visitation, but with my kids, it's so hard to find baby-sitting," Jeannette said. "If I can work it out, I'll let you know." She hung up the phone.

Mona sat across from Jeannette with her two toddlers. "If you really want to do hospital visitation, I can watch your kids for you sometimes."

"Would you? Thanks, Mona! You're a great friend," Jeannette smiled. She held her two-year-old in her arms. "Sometimes I wish you didn't have to work full-time so we could trade baby-sitting more often. I like being a stay-at-home mom, but would also like to get back into my church ministries and even try some new ones."

"Maybe there are other sources of baby-sitting besides moms," Mona suggested. She stroked her three-year-old's head. "If you do hospital visitation during the week, some of the college students at church who don't have classes every day might be available to watch your kids."

"I never thought of that," Jeannette said. "They could probably use some extra money."

"And they may not even want to be paid if you tell them you need baby-sitting so you can volunteer. They may see it as a ministry of their own," Mona said.

"I'll ask around," Jeannette said. She put her child down on the floor. "I wish my parents or my husband's parents lived in the area. They would love to spend more time with their grandchildren."

"There might be senior citizens at church who wouldn't mind being 'grandparents-for-a-day' to your kids. If they're retired, they may have time during the day," Mona suggested.

"That's a thought. Perhaps I can ask Ethel or Athena. They like children and I can easily pick them up in my van."

"Another mother might like to do hospital visitation. Maybe you could trade off baby-sitting with her and go every other week instead of each week," Mona said.

"I guess it doesn't hurt to ask. I just have to get up the nerve to do the asking," Jeannette confessed.

"It all starts with a phone call," Mona said as she pointed to the phone next to Jeannette.

Would you like to volunteer but have trouble finding child care? Don't be afraid to ask for help. Nehemiah asked the king for letters introducing him to people who would give him safe conduct and building supplies. He didn't know those people personally, but the king probably did. In the same way, we may have to ask others for referrals.

Loving Father, thank you for my family. I know I am serving you by taking care of them, but I also have a desire to serve you in the church. Help me to find capable people to care for my kids so I can also work for you outside the home.

I Can't Find the Receipt

The wicked borrow and do not repay,
but the righteous give generously.

Psalm 37:21

Bonus Reading: Psalm 37:25–26; 112:5

Trent and Janaya love gardening. Friends marvel at their backyard. Brightly colored foliage surrounds a pond with a recycling waterfall. The couple barbeques on a built-in outdoor grill. Friends and family enjoy their meals and the scenery from a quiet gazebo. People go to Trent and Janaya for advice on their own backyards.

When the church moved into a new building, the leaders asked them to landscape the front. They eagerly took on the responsibility. However, when they were told they had only so much to spend, their hearts fell. They really wanted to do something nice. After discussing it, the couple decided to use some of their own money and donate it to the church. They never told anyone how much extra they spent.

The first Sunday after everything had been planted, the parishioners oohed and aahed. Freshly laid sod created a green carpet visible from the street. Young hostas, colorful impatiens, and elephant's ear flanked the stone path leading from the parking lot to the front entrance. Boston ivy began its climb up the two columns on both sides of the door. A mix of azaleas underscored the stained glass windows. Brightly colored perennials greeted churchgoers as they entered the building.

The head deacon asked them how much extra they spent. Trent said, "Not much. I'll just take it off on my taxes as a charitable deduction."

"The church will reimburse you for your expenses. The council allotted more money than I first thought."

"That's okay. Just consider it a donation. I'll turn in receipts up to the original amount."

When the couple got home, they looked for all the receipts. They only found half of them. Trent said, "Now we can't get reimbursed for one-fourth of what the church was willing to pay for and we'll get no tax deduction at all."

"Don't worry about it. We spent twice as much on our own backyard. It's for the Lord," Janaya reminded him.

Janaya and Trent were not selfish with their finances when it came to the church. They willingly spent their own money to buy plants for the churchgoers' enjoyment. They donated as to the Lord and not to men.

Dear God, thank you for the finances you have allowed me to accumulate. May I never be selfish or self-serving with them. Help me to give willingly and cheerfully to your work.

Face Down!

His disciples asked him what this parable meant.

Luke 8:9

Bonus Reading: Luke 8:4–15

"Class, it's time for our coloring contest," Miss Quan announced.

"Hurray!" shouted Danny.

"All right!" exclaimed Melissa.

"I'm gonna win," said Jessi.

"Quiet down, class! Let's clear the table," Miss Quan instructed. You will have ten minutes. To be fair, keep your coloring pictures face down until I say go." She distributed the papers one by one.

As she passed by Carson on her way to the crayon can, his paper lay face up. He sat staring at a poster on the wall. *That's odd,* she thought. *He's usually so obedient. Maybe he wasn't listening.*

Miss Quan turned back to look at Carson. "Face down," she reminded.

Carson immediately bent forward and put his face down on top of the table.

Fighting back a chuckle, Miss Quan gently lifted Carson by the shoulders and placed him upright again. She turned his paper face down and placed the can in the middle of the table. She looked up at the clock and at the precise moment announced, "You may begin."

Although we think we are communicating clearly, others may still misunderstand us. Because Carson wasn't listening the first time, he didn't know "face down" referred to his paper, not his actual face. Jesus taught in parables. The disciples didn't always understand what he meant, so they asked Jesus to clarify. It is important for us today to communicate clearly and to make sure we comprehend what others say and mean. Church ministries need open lines of communication.

We must choose our words carefully and, more importantly, avoid overreacting until we understand clearly what others mean.

Holy Speaker, help me to communicate my ideas clearly and honestly and to really listen when others are giving theirs. Let me not rely on hearsay, but speak directly with the source. Help me to think before I speak and not hurt others with my words.

Thank You

Man is tested by the praise he receives.

Proverbs 27:21

Bonus Reading: Luke 18:9–14

Perry and Shawn uttered their last words of the Christmas sketch. As they walked off in their biblical costumes, the stagehand whispered, "Great job!"

Perry shook off his hood and replied, "It was nothing."

Shawn smiled and said, "Thank you."

While they walked toward the changing room, a woman came up to them laughing and said, "That last joke really killed me!"

"No, it didn't," Perry laughed back.

Shawn just smiled.

The two arrived at the changing room. The drama team captain grinned at them as he held out his hand. He grabbed their hands and shook them hard as they walked through the door. "I really want to thank you two for doing the sketch. It was a stupendous performance!"

"Praise the Lord," Perry breezed.

Shawn nodded and said, "Thank you."

As the men changed out of their costumes, Perry remarked, "I was really 'on' today. I sure nailed the timing on that last joke. Did you hear everyone laughing? I had 'em rollin' in the aisles! Pardon the expression. Ha-ha!"

Shawn nodded and said, "Yep."

"What's wrong with you? You've hardly said anything since we got offstage. Didn't you think we did good?" Perry asked.

Shawn replied, "God did good."

When people praise us for doing a good job at church, sometimes we reply with the right Christian cliché or downplay our performance to make people think that we are humble when in reality we are proud of ourselves. In Jesus' parable about the Pharisee and the tax collector who both went up to the temple, the Pharisee prayed to show others how good he was. The tax collector recognized his own sin and begged for mercy. The tax collector went home justified before God.

It is not wrong to feel good about doing well, but we need to remember that God is the One who gives us our abilities and blesses our efforts. Instead of trying to project humility, sometimes a simple thank-you will do.

Bestower of Blessings, thank you for giving me my abilities. If I accomplish anything, it is because of your mercy and grace. Help me to see myself as you do and to have the proper perspective. Please bless my efforts done for your glory.

From Jealousy to Worship

But Moses replied, "Are you jealous for my sake? I wish that all the LORD's people were prophets and that the LORD would put his Spirit on them!"

Numbers 11:29

Bonus Reading: Numbers 11:24–29

Lynnette spied Elise at the front of the sanctuary. As the congregation filed out of the pews, Lynnette pushed upstream to meet Elise halfway down the aisle. "I've been meaning to talk to you," she said. "Our small group is starting up again this month and I was wondering if you might be interested in checking it out."

Elise hesitated. "Um, I don't think so. My baby is still too young to bring to a group like that. Maybe when she's older."

"That's okay. I'll check back with you next year."

As a Bible study leader, Lynnette tried to recruit new members to her small group each September. She had hoped some of the younger women would join. Everyone she talked to declined. After a couple of years of asking with no success, Lynnette gave up.

The next year Lynnette found out secondhand that Audrey had started a mothers group and the very same women she had asked several times had joined Audrey's study. Questions whirled through her mind. *What's wrong with my group? Why did they join hers and not mine? Why didn't anyone tell me this new group was starting?* The green-eyed monster began to rear its ugly head.

Then the Holy Spirit spoke to Lynnette. *Be glad the new group began. Perhaps it meets those mothers' particular needs better than your group. They didn't join any of the other existing womens groups either. Don't take it personally.*

Lynnette prayed. *God, forgive me for being jealous, even for a second. I am truly happy Audrey started the new group. Those mothers have a good role model to look up to. Perhaps they feel more comfort-*

able sharing among their peers. Help their group to grow spiritually and closer to each other.

Lynnette determined to commend Audrey the next time she saw her for taking on the responsibility of shepherding the moms.

You can turn jealousy into worship. Thank God for the object of your envy. Thank him for the abilities and assets of that person. Then thank him for your talents and ministry.

> *Father, you know me better than anyone. You understand how many times I have to say "No!" to jealous thoughts. Turn my mind from them to whatever is excellent or praiseworthy.*

Me? A Project Leader?

Moses said to God, "Who am I, that I should go to Pharaoh and bring the Israelites out of Egypt? And God said, "I will be with you."

Exodus 3:11–12

Bonus Reading: Psalm 89:47

Marlon's pastor asked him to head the stewardship campaign team. Before deciding, he considered how much time he could devote each week to the campaign, taking into account his job, home, and other church duties. He asked the church leadership what their goals for the campaign were. He mulled over how he could best reach those goals and listed objectives to accomplish them. He thought of others he could ask to serve on his team whose strengths would complement and contrast with his own. After much prayer and contemplation, he finally accepted the position.

Marlon figured he could spend five hours per week working on the campaign and stuck with that schedule as much as possible. He began calling potential teammates or speaking with them in person after church services. Without scaring them off, he relayed their basic duties and a general time frame so they would know what they would be getting into. After assembling his team, he typed up notes for his first meeting.

He wanted his teammates to feel comfortable, so they met at his home in the living room. He passed out the notes so they could follow along as he briefly reviewed the goals and objectives of the campaign. He drew their attention to a page that listed each person's duties with a more detailed time frame. He asked for their feedback. He turned to the budget page and asked them if it was sufficient for them to accomplish their objectives.

Before everyone left, they set a date for the next meeting. Marlon asked them for their e-mail addresses to keep in contact. He recommended that they ask for e-mail addresses of the people they solicited for help. As he said good-bye, Marlon reassured them that he would give them the support they needed to accomplish their tasks.

Has your pastor asked you to head a special project? You want to say yes but are not sure you have the time, expertise, or people skills to pull it off. First ask yourself, "Have I counted the cost?" Then remember, "I just keep trusting my Lord."

Loving Lord, I believe you want me to lead a special project. Give me the clarity of mind to arrange my schedule to accommodate it. Help me keep my priorities straight and choose the right people to help me. Enable me to make the best use of my time.

Limited Faith

If you have faith as small as a mustard seed, you can say to this mountain, "Move from here to there" and it will move. Nothing will be impossible for you.

Matthew 17:20

Bonus Reading: Matthew 17:14–20

"It's impossible. We can never do it," Marcel insisted.

"Yes, we can. Where's your faith?" Chandra countered.

Marcel put his hands to the sides of his head. A waitress placed their pizza on the table. "It's not a question of faith," Marcel said. "It's a matter of practicality."

Chandra reached for a slice of pepperoni. "What's so impractical about trying to reach teens for Christ in a place they normally go?"

"In the mall? Are you crazy?" Marcel whispered loudly. He looked around the pizzeria, but no one was paying attention to them. "There's got to be a gazillion rules against preaching in the mall."

"We won't be preaching. Our band will be entertaining the crowd with music that just happens to have Christian lyrics. They'll love your voice," Chandra said as she put down her slice. "Besides, I've heard Christmas carolers in the mall sing 'Joy to the World.'"

Marcel looked at his pizza and shook his head. "They won't let us give a testimony. No one's going to listen anyway."

"We're not gonna spout Bible verses or use a lot of Christian jargon. In fact, we can make up a modern-day parable. Who can object to a story?"

Marcel rolled his eyes. "I simply say it's not going to work."

"What's the harm in asking? All the management can say is no," Chandra said.

Marcel reached into his jacket and pulled out a cell phone. He handed it to Chandra. "Be my guest."

Chandra called information and waited to be connected. "Hi, may I speak with the mall manager?"

Do you feel God leading you to serve him in an unusual way? One that stretches your faith and makes you leave your comfort zone? Remember, nothing is impossible with God.

Dear God, you have a task for me to do and I'm not sure I'm up to it. I feel like I have no faith. In my head, I know you can do the impossible, but my heart doesn't believe it. Change my heart, Lord.

Getting to Know You

A new command I give you: Love one another. As I have loved you, so you must love one another. By this all men will know that you are my disciples, if you love one another.

John 13:34–35

Bonus Reading: Ephesians 4:25, 32

Ramona had been directing the youth choir for five years. In that span of time, she had seen children grow into youth and youth mature into adulthood. Each August, the church showed its appreciation for volunteer leaders of ministries. This year, they interviewed a series of churchgoers, asking what they appreciated about various leaders. The videotaped interviews were shown to the congregation as part of Sunday worship. Youth choir members said the following about Ramona:

"Ramona always makes her expectations clear to us. She's also willing to spend extra time with us if we need help learning our parts."

"Ramona is sensitive to other people's feelings. One time I came in too early on a song and was the only one singing for a whole measure. She didn't yell at me."

"She spends time with us outside of practice. After Christmas, she had the whole choir over to her house for a dessert party. She even made all the goodies!"

"Ramona is a very open person. When she makes a mistake, she admits it. She's willing to let you see the 'real' Ramona."

"I don't want to leave youth choir when I 'age out.' Ramona makes it so fun."

"Ramona has taught me a lot about music and worshiping God through singing. I hope someday I can be a friend to someone like she's been to me."

"We love you, Ramona!"

Ramona invested a lot of time building relationships with her choir members, as evidenced in their responses. She discipled these young people to become more Christlike. Ramona may have had to work at being so loving and giving. In the same way, if you are not naturally a "people person" you may need to train yourself to be more open and friendly to others, especially to those volunteers under your leadership.

Lover of all humankind, help me to nurture others with your love. Help me to make disciples by building close relationships with the people with whom I serve. May I become a catalyst for their Christian growth.

Doing God's Business

> But select capable men from all the people—men who fear God, trustworthy men who hate dishonest gain—and appoint them as officials over thousands, hundreds, fifties and tens. Have them serve as judges for the people at all times, but have them bring every difficult case to you; the simple cases they can decide themselves. That will make your load lighter, because they will share it with you.
>
> Exodus 18:21–22

Bonus Reading: Exodus 18:13–26

Conrad and Justine were photocopying notes for the upcoming business meeting in three weeks. "I'm glad they decided to streamline the sessions," Justine said. "I had a hard time keeping my baby quiet for three hours."

"I agree. I'd rather read all this information at my own leisure before the meeting rather than sit there and listen to someone else read it out loud," Conrad said. "Receiving it ahead of time helps people come prepared—not only for the main session, but for the premeeting the week before."

Justine reloaded the copy machine. "I like the premeeting. Not everyone is interested in all my questions, so I don't feel bad for wasting lots of other people's time. Since a relative few show up, I don't feel as intimidated asking questions as I would in a huge group."

"I feel more prepared to vote intelligently when I've had time to think about the answers to my questions," Conrad added.

"I think the questions raised at the premeeting help the leaders prepare to explain the complex issues at the main one. People can still ask questions there too, but there are less of them. Too many questions bog us down," Justine said, shaking her head.

Conrad took a stack of projected budget sheets from the machine. "I know it's hard on the accountants to get all these numbers together. Sometimes the financial statements can't be given out till the last minute." He turned and pointed at the stacks on the table waiting to be packaged. "But the minutes of the last meeting, pastor's report, elders' report, church directory—these are relatively easy to give out ahead of time."

"As long as people can make the time to do it early," Justine said, laughing.

The two proceeded to assemble the packets into envelopes, which would be passed out for the next two Sundays.

Do business meetings last forever at your church? What can you do to streamline the process? Moses' father-in-law, Jethro, suggested he appoint men to help him judge the Israelites, thus lightening his load and enabling the people to receive justice in a shorter period of time. God wants us to use our time and resources wisely. Perhaps you can even increase attendance at meetings if they are shorter.

Dear God, help me be prepared to participate in church business meetings. Give our leaders wisdom to conduct them in an efficient and timely manner.

Time Control

Be very careful, then, how you live—not as unwise but as wise, making the most of every opportunity, because the days are evil.

Ephesians 5:15–16

Bonus Reading: Colossians 4:5

Colleen waved to the class of English students as they filed out the door. "Good-bye, Mr. Li. Good-bye, Mrs. Gutierrez. See you Wednesday, Mrs. Hamamoto! Practice those conversation exercises, Mr. Parisi."

Colleen volunteered as a teacher's assistant twice a week in the English As a Second Language class at her church. She helped the students practice their conversation skills and corrected papers for the teacher. She enjoyed interacting with the students and seeing them improve.

The teacher handed her a stack of papers. "Can you correct these at home tonight?" she asked.

Colleen eyed the stack. "I'll try my best," she swallowed.

That night at home, Colleen placed the papers on top of two other piles of English class exercises sitting on the kitchen table. *I've got to correct those tonight,* she said to herself. She shuffled toward the stairs and eyed the mounds of books and magazines that lined the edges of each step. *Gotta clean those up,* she thought as she trudged up the stairs. She opened her bedroom door. A mountain of clean laundry greeted her on her bed. *I've got to fold those clothes someday,* she reminded herself. Some socks fell onto the floor as she flopped down on the edge of the bed. "So many things to do! I don't know where to begin!" she groaned aloud.

Do you wish you had ten extra hours a day to catch up with all your work? Perhaps you need to buy a day planner or make a to-do list prioritizing what needs to be done when. Colleen needs to fold the clothes tonight so she can sleep in her bed. She needs to correct some of the papers tonight and some tomorrow night before class on Wednesday. She can hold off on the magazines and books until she has guests over. With our busy lives, learning to manage our time is essential.

Father, time has gotten away from me. Help me figure out where it's all going and how to make the best use of each day. Let me not put it off till tomorrow.

Keep Your Volunteers

I thank God, whom I serve, as my forefathers did, with a clear conscience, as night and day I constantly remember you in my prayers.

2 Timothy 1:3

Bonus Reading: 1 Thessalonians 5:9–11

Luke handed Tristan a new digital camera. Tristan turned it over in his hands. "Thanks, Luke. I'll be really careful with this. I know the church paid a lot of money for it."

"I trust you, Tristan. You're the newsletter's best photographer," Luke said. "You're going to the church anniversary celebration on Saturday, right?"

"Got it down on my calendar. Any particular pictures you want, Boss?"

"Anything that shows it's the church anniversary, not some other function. Use your best judgment."

Tristan played with the buttons. "Do I have to learn how to download pictures?"

"No, just give me the camera as soon as you're done and I'll figure it out. I know you're busy with your new baby, and there are several ministries that will want these shots right away." Luke held up his fingers and counted. "Besides our newsletter, there's the church web site, PowerPoint slides for next Sunday's service, the bulletin board—your work will be famous!" Luke laughed.

Tristan chuckled. "I'm glad the church was willing to invest in such a useful tool. I feel good knowing they appreciate and support our work."

Luke clapped him on the back. "I appreciate you, too." He drew Tristan closer and lowered his voice. "I've been praying for you and your family. Now that you've got two little ones, if you or your wife ever need anything . . ."

"Oh, we're fine," Tristan began, "but there is one thing I need."

"Name it."

"The instructions for the camera."

Volunteers need to feel they have the backing of their leaders and the church. Telling them that they are doing a good job and that you are willing to assist them will go a long way in retaining your helpers. Prayer support and an adequate budget are also ways leaders can uphold their volunteers. Lack of encouragement is a major reason some Christians quit ministries.

Lord, thank you for those who serve with me. Help me to support them in their part of the ministry. Show me how to encourage them to keep serving you.

Let Go of Your Talents

As the eyes of slaves look to the hand of their master,
    as the eyes of a maid look to the hand of her mistress,
so our eyes look to the Lord our God,
    till he shows us his mercy.

Psalm 123:2

Bonus Reading: Psalm 123

Whitney painted a mural of animals frolicking in the wild on the church nursery walls. Above the baptistery, she created a beautiful mountain lake surrounded by verdant trees.

In September, the producer of the Christmas program came up to her. "Whitney, your murals are so lovely. You have a great talent for painting."

Whitney smiled. "Why, thank you, Kira. You're so kind."

"I was wondering," Kira began, "if you might consider helping us out with the Christmas program. We need someone to paint a backdrop of a biblical city night skyline. It's for a very important scene in our play this year."

Whitney pursed her lips. "One scene? How big does this have to be?"

"It will fill the entire stage from left to right."

Whitney shook her head. "I'm sorry, I don't think I have time to paint something so big that will only be used for one scene."

"But we can use it again next year or the year after," Kira said. "And many new people will come to the play."

Whitney put on her best sad face. "I am really sorry, but I can't do it. Why don't you ask one of the young people?"

As Kira walked away, Whitney thought, *Paint something that big that may only be seen once a year, if that? Not worth my time!*

Whitney only wanted to use her painting talents on permanent projects like the nursery or baptistery where lots of people would see them all the time. She closed herself to the idea that her gift could be used to help bring in Christ-seekers. In Psalm 123, the servant is submissive to the master. We must lay our gifts completely in our Master's hand, ready to use them in whatever way he leads us. We must not hold back and use them only when we feel like it.

Master, I lay my all on your altar. I know that seeing an open door itself does not always mean you want me to walk through it. But help me to be willing to seize the right opportunities to serve you. Help me not to be so narrow-minded in the scope of my service that I miss chances to make a difference in your kingdom.

A Servant's Spirit

"Drink, my lord," she said, and quickly lowered the jar to her hands and gave him a drink.

Genesis 24:18

Bonus Reading: Genesis 24:17–21

"Thanks for the copies," the Sunday school teacher said as she left the church office.

"Thanks, Margaret," the pastor said as he took his class notes.

Margaret closed the lid of the photocopier. Teachers and staff had been coming in all morning requesting copies for their classes. Time to add up Sunday school attendance. Before she left that afternoon, Margaret prepared roll sheets for the next quarter.

As her brother Seth drove them both home, he teased, "Did you meet any interesting guys in the copy room today?"

Margaret punched him on the arm. "Very funny."

"Seriously, when are you going to try a real ministry, where you can interact with people?" Seth asked as he merged onto the freeway.

Margaret glared at Seth. "I have a 'real' ministry. Lots of people depend on me to provide materials for their Sunday school kids. I help them know who's new and who needs to be followed up on. Helping out with Sunday school administration fits me just fine."

"I didn't mean to say what you're doing isn't important," Seth quickly added. "Of course it is. All churches need people to play behind-the-scenes roles. Not everybody feels led to be out in front of others."

"It's not that I'm shy or can't do anything else. Remember when I was in the Christmas play? I just feel that right now this is where God has led me to serve him."

"And you're doing a great job," Seth encouraged. "You're right— you need to be where God has called you."

As they drove into the garage, Margaret said with a twinkle in her eye, "I did meet a girl today who I think would be perfect for you."

Administrative positions are very important to any ministry. Pastors, teachers, worship teams, and other leaders depend a lot on those who are behind the scenes preparing the way for them. No matter what ministry you are called to, it is important to have a servant's heart. When we serve others, we are actually serving God.

> *God, thank you that I can serve in a behind-the-scenes role. Help me to do my part so that others can do theirs for your glory.*

A Place to Belong

If you have any encouragement from being united with Christ . . .
then make my joy complete by being like-minded, having the same
love, being one in spirit and purpose.

Philippians 2:1–2

Bonus Reading: Philippians 2:1–5; Proverbs 27:17

Myles loved to attend choir practice. A usually quiet fellow, he came alive when surrounded by God's people singing praises to the Lord. The choir members became his second family. Each section sat together during rehearsals. He was leader of the basses. More than any other ministry that he had been involved with, he felt choir was "his place."

That is, until the choir director moved on to another church. A new director was hired who made some changes. First of all, he required that everyone re-audition. Because they were short on tenors, he moved Myles to that section. "You have great potential," he explained to Myles.

One night after rehearsal, Myles and Sam were walking to their cars. When Sam asked how singing in the tenor section was going, Myles couldn't stand being quiet any longer. "I miss you guys. The tenors are okay, but I don't know them very well. Singing tenor is hard. I can't sight-read as fast and those high notes are killing me. Now that I'm not a section leader, I feel like I'm at the bottom of the heap." They arrived at Myles's car. He looked around for eavesdroppers. "You wanna know how I really feel? I'm mad at that new director for making me switch. I just wanna quit."

Taken aback, Sam urged, "Don't quit. You'll get used to singing tenor." He put his hand on Myles's shoulder and looked him straight in the eye. "You are still a very valuable member of this team. Don't worry that you can't sing like you did as a bass. God still accepts your praise to him." He took his hand off Myles's shoulder. "Give the new director a chance."

Myles stayed in choir. Eventually, he became a good tenor. He got to know the other men in his section better and enjoyed fellowshipping with them. By switching parts, he actually widened his circle of friends. He never became a section leader, but it didn't bother him. As he got to know the new director, he found out he wasn't such a bad fellow after all.

Myles "rediscovered" his niche in God's service. We all crave that feeling of belonging. Being part of a team gives us a sense of camaraderie and the encouragement we need to persevere. "Iron sharpens iron" as we seek to improve or expand our service for him.

Heavenly Father, thank you for giving me the opportunity to serve you in the church. Thank you for those who serve with me and help me to become the best I can be for you. I am especially grateful for the brothers and sisters who have encouraged me when I have felt like quitting.

Great Job!

Now Moses said to Hobab . . . "We are setting out for the place about which the LORD said, 'I will give it to you.' Come with us and we will treat you well, for the LORD has promised good things to Israel . . . Please do not leave us. You know where we should camp in the desert, and you can be our eyes. If you come with us, we will share with you whatever good things the LORD gives us."

Numbers 10:29, 31-32

Bonus Reading: Numbers 10:29–33

Mallory helped raise money for the church by compiling a recipe book every three years. It was sold at church, on the church web site, and in local bookstores. Church attendees contributed their favorite original recipes for a variety of dishes ranging from entrees to desserts. Mallory wanted to show her personal appreciation for each of their efforts and for the work of those who helped with the layout and printing of the book, marketing, and distribution.

Mallory used some blank recipe cards to write thank-you notes. She filled small cellophane bags with candy and tied them with ribbon. She punched a hole in the card and threaded it onto the ribbon before tying the final bow. She placed them all in a shopping bag to bring to church.

Before service, Mallory passed out as many of her treats as she could to the contributors, smiling and saying a personal thank-you. When she gave one to Geneva, Geneva said, "You're always so thoughtful, Mallory. I don't mind at all helping you with each book."

Saving the rest for after service, Mallory took her seat in the auditorium. Before the pastor came up to deliver the sermon, the head deacon walked up to the podium.

"Would all those who had a part in putting together the recipe book please stand?" the deacon asked. Several parishioners stood up, Mallory included. "To show our thanks, let's give them a round of applause." Mallory and the others smiled as the congregation clapped.

As they sat down, the deacon said, "Mallory and her crew did a fine job. I bought my copy already!" The audience laughed as he held up the volume. "After service, the books will be available at the Welcome Center."

Personal and corporate thanks go a long way in retaining volunteers. People liked working with Mallory and felt valued when their efforts were acknowledged by her and the church. Moses complimented Hobab on his desert skills when he asked him to accompany the Israelites to the Promised Land. When people know they are appreciated, they are more likely to stay with a ministry or a church.

> *Everlasting Father, I thank you for the people who serve with me. Without their help, the ministry could not continue. Help me to show my appreciation for them.*

Why Volunteer?

All a man's ways seem right to him,
but the LORD weighs the heart.

Proverbs 21:2

Bonus Reading: Proverbs 16:2

Armand grinned as Dylan walked through the door. "Welcome to the gift-wrapping party!"

"Glad to be here," Dylan said. "I think this Angel Tree project is great. The kids will be so happy to get these presents from their parents in prison. Thanks for giving people like me an opportunity to make a difference."

Armand clapped him on the shoulder. "You're on my delivery team." As Dylan made his way into the sea of wrapping paper, Armand turned to welcome other volunteers. "Gina, so glad to see you!"

"I finished all my Christmas shopping early, so I had a free Saturday. I figured you needed the help," Gina said. She held up a brown paper bag. "I brought my own scissors!"

Armand chuckled. He walked over to where the Turner family sat on the floor. A plastic garbage bag filled with unwrapped gifts lay beside them. He bent down to help the daughter tie a bow on the present she just finished wrapping. "How's it going, Pumpkin?"

"Wrapping is fun!" she said.

By the end of the afternoon, twelve bags of wrapped gifts lay near the door. Armand gave last minute instructions to the delivery teams who would also be sharing the gospel with the prisoners' families. As he picked up one of the bags, he breathed a silent prayer. *God, help me to bless a family today like you blessed mine when I was . . . in jail.*

People have many good reasons to volunteer. Praise God for all of them! Their level of commitment may rise with their motivation. Armand was in charge because he had personally experienced the benefits of the program. Dylan agreed to not only wrap gifts, but also be on a delivery team because he wanted to make a difference. Gina used her free time in a place where she saw a need. The little girl thought it was fun, but the parents may also have wanted to teach her compassion for others less fortunate. If you are a leader, you need to find out what motivates your people and match them with appropriate volunteer positions. You may also need to teach them biblical reasons for serving.

Dear Lord, I cannot judge other people's hearts. But I pray that I will have proper motivations for serving you. Help me to encourage spiritual reasons for service in others.

Staying in My Rut

We hear that some among you are idle . . . never tire of doing what is right.

2 Thessalonians 3:11, 13

Bonus Reading: 2 Thessalonians 3:6–13

Seraphina waved good-bye to her kindergartener on the first day of school in September. As she left the room, she began humming, "It's the Most Wonderful Time of the Year." She thought to herself, *I'm free, I'm free. At least until 12:30.*

For the first week, Seraphina relaxed at home during the time her son was in school. She curled up on the sofa with a novel she had been meaning to read all year. She drank hot cocoa and ate candy as she turned the pages of her book.

The second week, Seraphina began to feel guilty about all her free time and did a little housework as she listened to her favorite CDs. She washed dishes and cleaned up the kitchen. Then she read her novel.

By the third week, Seraphina had gotten into a new routine. On Mondays she went grocery shopping. On Tuesdays she did the laundry. On Wednesdays she went to the library. On Thursdays she cleaned the bathrooms. On Fridays she went to the mall or rented a movie from the video store. Every day she read a book.

In November, her friend Alexis broke her routine by coming for a visit. As they sat at the kitchen counter drinking tea, Alexis mentioned her involvement in the Homebound Ministry.

"What exactly do you do?" Seraphina asked.

"Once a week, people in the church make and deliver meals for shut-ins. Sometimes we stay and chat with the homebound. We make enough food for lunch and dinner," Alexis explained.

"Sounds like a worthwhile ministry," Seraphina commented thoughtfully as she sipped her tea.

"How would you like to join us? Sometimes you don't even have to make the meal, just deliver it."

Seraphina stopped mid-sip. She put her cup down on the counter. "I don't know. I'm pretty busy at home." She began naming off the things she did.

Alexis smiled. "I do most of those things too. But I need a little excitement in my life. Just consider it a nice break from your usual routine."

Seraphina sighed. "I'll have to think about it. I just got used to my son being in school every morning. I suppose it's easier to stay home in a rut than to go out and volunteer."

"You'd really be making a difference in the shut-ins' lives. They *have* to stay home, but you can go anywhere you want," Alexis said.

"That's true. I'll let you know what I decide on Sunday."

Have you been asked to serve the Lord in a particular ministry? Seraphina could easily fit the Homebound Ministry into her routine, but even admitted her hesitancy was due to her own laziness.

Dear God, I feel a need to serve you in a certain area, but I'm so stuck in my own routine that I find it hard to change. Give me the gumption to get up and just do it.

The Greater Love

No servant can serve two masters. Either he will hate the one and love the other, or he will be devoted to the one and despise the other. You cannot serve both God and Money.

Luke 16:13

Bonus Reading: Exodus 20:3–4

Ernest felt like he had won the lottery! A fireworks company had just donated the means to put on a half-hour show for a Fourth of July outdoor concert. Ernest's church, along with several others in the area, worked together each year to reach out to the city and provide this community service.

Ernest choreographed fireworks shows for a living, so when he heard about this opportunity he felt like a kid in a candy store. A half hour to create anything he wanted! Unlimited creative control! Money not a problem! Ernest loved his job and he was more than willing to use his professional skills on a church project. He began to plan his show.

The Fourth of July celebration committee met to discuss the program. Representatives from all the churches attended this meeting. Ernest eagerly brought his plans.

The chairman passed out a tentative schedule of events. Ernest scanned the page for the fireworks show. When he found it at the bottom of the page, he could not believe his eyes.

"Excuse me, there must be some mistake. The fireworks company donated supplies for a half-hour show and this schedule says it's only ten minutes."

"There's no mistake," the chairman explained. "With so many organizations participating, each one has only ten minutes. I've already spoken with the owner of the company and he understands our situation."

Ernest stood up. "But I've already planned a half-hour show. I have the description right here. It's going to be great! I'm ordering special rockets. The music and the rockets are going to fit perfectly with one another. It ends with a cross and an American flag. The audience will be dazzled and amazed!"

The chairman stifled a laugh. "Ernest, please sit down. I know you're really excited about your show, but let's not forget why we're doing this. The fireworks will bring the people in. Besides seeing the display, they need to hear the gospel. We have a great opportunity to share Christ with our community through music and preaching. And we have to be fair to all the churches by giving each one equal time."

Ernest sat down. Throughout the rest of the meeting he silently fumed. *My fireworks share the gospel, just in a different way. I bet everyone would rather see the fireworks than hear somebody preach. They don't understand what great art I produce. Nobody understands me.*

Ernest went home and reluctantly altered his plans. The celebration was a huge success, and everyone wanted to have fireworks again the following year, but Ernest refused to participate.

Ernest loved his craft more than he loved God. He thought his fireworks were more important than the reason for having the show in the first place. Sometimes Christians will volunteer in a certain area because they love doing it. But will love for an activity sustain them when they face relational conflict or other adverse conditions? Good works are worth nothing if not coupled with love for God and people.

Seeker of my heart, I want to love you more than anything else, including my church activities. May I never put what I want to do before what you want me to do.

Weary in Well-Doing

"Martha, Martha," the Lord answered, "you are worried and upset about many things, but only one thing is needed. Mary has chosen what is better, and it will not be taken away from her."

Luke 10:41–42

Bonus Reading: 2 Thessalonians 3:13

"Vicki, I'd like to help you, but I'm going to have to pass on this special singing ensemble," Lila said, balancing the phone on her shoulder. She gave little Tommy to her husband Dan.

"But we need you! You're so talented and I don't know of anyone else," Vicki pleaded.

"Let me think about it for a few days," Lila replied. She hung up and turned to Dan. "I hate it when people think I have all the time in the world just because I'm a stay-at-home mom. Then I feel bad when I say no."

"You're already doing a lot for the church besides caring for this little guy," said Dan as he put Tommy in his high chair. "You sing in the choir, baby-sit, and teach Sunday school. You don't want to burn out."

"But I hate to disappoint people," Lila sighed. "Vicki's a good friend."

"Then she should understand your situation."

Lila brought Tommy his cereal. "If I could think of someone else who might be willing to sing, maybe I won't feel so bad for saying no."

"That's a great idea!" Dan put down his tea. "How about Marianne? She sings the same part as you."

"She might be available," Lila said as she gave Tommy his milk bottle. "Vicki doesn't know Marianne very well, but I'll recommend her."

"And even if she's not available, stick to your decision about saying no. Vicki will understand."

"I hope so. But what if she doesn't?"

"It's God you're responsible to, not Vicki."

Do you ever feel burnt out by all your church activities? Take a moment to evaluate your priorities. Ask God to show you which ministries to keep and which you need to cut out. God doesn't want us to tire of doing right, but neither does he want us to keep going nonstop. When Jesus visited Mary and Martha, he gently reminded Martha to slow down and be more like Mary. Serving God was good, but listening to him was better.

In whatever areas we serve him, we ought to be able to give our best, even if we have to give up an area to spend more quality time in another. You needn't feel guilty about concentrating your efforts in specific ministries if it means doing a better job for God in each of them.

Dear Lord, help me say yes to what is most important to you. Give me wisdom to know and courage to say no at the right time.

Too Busy to Worship

> Yet a time is coming and has now come when the true worshipers will worship the Father in spirit and truth, for they are the kind of worshipers the Father seeks. God is spirit, and his worshipers must worship in spirit and in truth.
>
> John 4:23–24

Bonus Reading: John 4:1–24

Jeannette rushed through the door of the sanctuary ten minutes late. *Oh no, they're already singing. I shouldn't have pushed the snooze button so many times.* She grabbed a bulletin from the usher and sat down to catch her breath. While the others sang, she glanced at the announcements and then checked her makeup. As she put her mirror away, the teal and mauve of the woman's skirt in front of her caught her attention. *What a combination,* she thought. *I would never wear that.*

During the message, Jeannette took out her Sunday school notes and studied them to prepare for teaching later that morning. Halfway through the sermon she put them away and tried to listen to the pastor. By the time she caught on, he was closing in prayer. She arose feeling very unsatisfied. *I never get anything out of the service,* she complained to herself.

Jeannette's body was at church, but her mind and spirit were far away. God demands true adoration from his followers, with our minds and hearts as well as our physical being. When Jesus spoke to the Samaritan woman at Jacob's well, he reminded her that the place of worship didn't matter as much as the worshiper's heart attitude.

Are you so busy doing things for the Lord on Sundays that exalting Christ with your heart takes second place? One might argue, "But serving God is part of worship." Perhaps we need to ask ourselves, "Are my activities for him preventing me from fully participating in and appreciating corporate worship?"

Look at the words of the songs as you honor God instead of singing from memory. Meditate on their meaning. Even while you drive to church, prepare your heart ahead of time, asking the Lord to speak to you that day. You will notice a big difference in your attitude.

Holy One, help me to worship you in spirit and in truth. Clear my mind of distracting thoughts. Cleanse my heart of unforgiveness. Let me sing freely to you and be ready to receive your message today.

Manage Anger with Love

Love is patient, love is kind. It does not envy, it does not boast, it is not proud. It is not rude, it is not self-seeking, it is not easily angered, it keeps no record of wrongs . . . it always protects, always trusts, always hopes, always perseveres. Love never fails.

1 Corinthians 13:4–5, 7–8

Bonus Reading: 1 Corinthians 13:1–13

Milo organized a trip to the botanical gardens for the senior citizens. As everyone disembarked from the bus, he noticed Efrem still on board. He walked back toward Efrem's seat.

"Is something the matter, Efrem?"

"I ain't gettin' off the bus."

"Why not?"

"I just ain't."

Milo tried to breathe slowly. "Now, Efrem, the driver is going to park the bus and lock it. It will get too hot inside for you to stay. I'll help you out." He reached for Efrem's arm.

Efrem pushed Milo away. "I kin get up myself."

As Milo backed away, Efrem slowly arose with the help of his cane. Milo stopped next to the driver's seat. As Efrem moseyed down the aisle, he waved Milo away. Milo shrugged and stepped off the bus to wait at the bottom step. Efrem held onto the rail, walked sideways down the stairs, then reached for the ground with his cane. With an exaggerated grunt, he stepped off the bus.

As Milo watched Efrem join the others, Milo's helper, Beatrice, walked up to him. "Is Efrem giving you a bad time again today?"

"He's just being his old cantankerous self. I pray before every senior outing for God to help me love him," sighed Milo.

"It's not easy to love someone as ornery as he is," Beatrice observed.

"Sometimes I want to give him a good shake. But of course you can't do that to old people," Milo laughed.

Beatrice chuckled. "I know what you mean. Only God can help us respond with kindness to someone like him."

Is someone in your life hard to love? In 1 Corinthians 13, *agape* love is described as a response more than a feeling. When we respond to a hard-to-love person with kindness, a soft word, or patience instead of rudeness or anger, we are showing him God's divine love. Only our Lord can give us the power to obey his commandment to love one another.

Lord of love, someone I know needs me to agape *him. Help me to react to him with kindness, support, and protection rather than anger, envy, or pride.*

Heart Reader

They said, "let this land be given to your servants as our possession. Do not make us cross the Jordan." Moses said to the Gadites and Reubenites, "Shall your countrymen go to war while you sit here?"

Numbers 32:5–6

Bonus Reading: Numbers 32:1–7, 14–19

"I knew that Abigail was up to something," Miriam hissed over the phone. "She wormed her way into the nominating committee again this year."

"I wouldn't put it that way," Chitra said. "Nobody else wanted to do it."

"Still, she's just going to make sure her friends' names are put on the ballot for the church elections. That's what happened last year. You know how it works. All the members suggest names and the committee decides whom to call to say they've been nominated. She's got real power there."

"She's not the only one on the committee. And besides, you don't know what she's thinking."

"Why are you on her side?"

"I'm not on anybody's side. I'm just saying it's dangerous to assign motives to people when you have no proof."

"I'll have all the proof I need when the ballot comes out," Miriam said as she hung up the phone.

A few weeks later, Miriam got a call from Abigail. "Guess what, Miriam? You've been nominated to serve on the finance team. Can I put your name on the ballot?"

Miriam was glad Abigail couldn't see her blush. "Um, I'll have to think about it," she squeaked. After clearing her voice she asked, "Who else was nominated?"

"The committee hasn't finished contacting everyone yet, but Carmela and Glynis said yes. The others said no. I don't know these two very well, but aren't they good friends of yours?"

"As a matter of fact they are," Miriam replied.

"If you have any questions as to what is required, I'd be glad to answer them," Abigail offered.

"No, I'm familiar with their duties. I'll get back to you by Sunday."

Miriam hung up the phone and sat down. She put her head in her hands and prayed, "Lord, forgive me for misjudging Abigail. I was wrong to say all those mean things about her. Chitra was right—I can't judge people's motives."

In the Bible, when the Reubenites and Gadites asked Moses if they could claim the land east of the Jordan River for their homes, Moses thought they had selfish motives and that they wouldn't help their brothers fight for the rest of the land. On the surface, it is not hard to see how Moses came to that conclusion. But in reality, the two tribes had pure motives and would not rest until their brothers were safe in the land. God is the only One who can look at the heart.

Dear Lord, forgive me for judging others. Help me to make sure my motives are pure and not worry about other people's motives.

Please Stay in Touch

What grieved [the Ephesians] most was [Paul's] statement that they would never see his face again.

Acts 20:38

Bonus Reading: Acts 20:31, 36–38

"I can't believe you're leaving," a deaf woman signed. She wept as she threw her arms around Loretta.

Loretta dried her own tears. She signed back, "I'll miss you. I'll miss everyone. But we'll still see each other at church. I'll drop by sometimes."

Loretta was leaving the deaf ministry. After four years of helping it grow, Loretta felt God was calling her to a different area of service. She had struggled with the decision, but sensed God's peace when she finally took the step.

The next Sunday, she stopped by the deaf service as they let out. She chatted with several parishioners, reminding them that she still prayed for them.

The following Christmas, she made some refreshments for the deaf ministry. She sent out cards to the ones to whom she was especially close. In the hallways, whenever she passed by former co-laborers in the ministry, she always smiled and said hello. During other church functions, she always asked how things were going in the deaf service.

As her other areas of service kept her busy, Loretta had less and less time to spend with the deaf. But she always found time to support their special meetings. Every year she attended their musical concert. She not only brought deaf friends, but hearing ones too. All of them enjoyed seeing the beautiful signing of the songs and watching colored lights dance with the music.

Loretta knew that she would have to let some relationships go as she forged new ones with others. But she knew that if she wanted to keep some of them, she would have to work at it.

Do you try to keep up relations with former co-laborers in Christ? If you have other common interests besides the particular ministry you served together in, you have a starting point. It is up to you and them to keep the fires of friendship going.

Ever-present Friend, I want to keep my friends, and hopefully they feel the same way. Help us to get together and become closer despite the infrequency of our meetings.

Is It Worth It?

I know your deeds, your love and faith, your service and perseverance, and that you are now doing more than you did at first.

Revelation 2:19

Bonus Reading: Numbers 11:4–9

"Good-bye, Eric!" Isabelle called out.

"See you in two weeks, Nina!" Rashid waved.

Isabelle closed the door of their town house. "I wish those two would hook up. They'd make a perfect couple."

Rashid put his arm around his wife. "Patience, dear. Matchmaking isn't the only reason we started the singles ministry." He held up his Bible and study guide.

"I know some people just want platonic relationships with both sexes. They enjoy the dinners and special outings," Isabelle said. "But I wish more people would make it a priority. I would love to see our group diminish in size because people have found their soul mates. But our problem is that we don't have a consistent core group. They come only when they have nothing better to do."

Rashid picked up paper cups and napkins from the coffee table. "Everyone's busy with their own lives. Most of them see each other on Sundays. They don't want to see them again on Fridays."

Isabelle followed Rashid to the kitchen with a plate of leftover cookies. "Sometimes I just wonder if it's worth it," she said.

Rashid threw the garbage in the trash can. He turned to Isabelle. "Look on the bright side. Platonic relationships have grown, the Bible study is making an impact on individual lives, and the outings are fun for those who attend." He picked up Isabelle's hand. "I think it is worth it."

Isabelle gave her husband a hug. "Thanks for trying to cheer me up." She released him and her face brightened. "Maybe we can arrange a joint meeting with a singles group from another church," she said.

"That would certainly raise interest. It's a great idea," Rashid agreed.

"In fact, I was just talking to someone at work whose church also has a small singles group. I can look into the possibility of us getting together," Isabelle said. She looked around the kitchen. "Where's my phone book? I can call her right now."

Do you find fulfillment in your volunteer position? If not, maybe you need to reflect on the positive results of your work. The Israelites complained about having to eat manna every day and yearned for the leeks and garlic of Egypt. But they forgot how oppressive the Egyptians were and how God miraculously led them out and provided for them. We will find our volunteering more fulfilling if we praise God for his blessings rather than concentrate on what we don't have. Then we can work on improving our ministry.

Dear God, I am getting discouraged in the work. I feel unfulfilled in the area I am serving in. Help me to remember your blessings and the good that has occurred through my efforts for you. Give me wisdom to improve the ministry.

Message over Messenger

My message and my preaching were not with wise and persuasive words, but with a demonstration of the Spirit's power, so that your faith might not rest on men's wisdom, but on God's power.

1 Corinthians 2:4–5

Bonus Reading: 1 Corinthians 2:1–5

Hunter loved making videos for the church. On holidays and other special occasions, you could count on watching an artfully done clip. Hunter read every video-making book and magazine and watched every instructional DVD he could get his hands on. His home office overflowed with VCRs, computers, digital cameras, and other paraphernalia.

Hunter's latest project was a video encouraging churchgoers to participate in the National Day of Prayer. "See you at the pole" was the catchphrase for Christians to gather at a flagpole to pray for the nation. Hunter had just bought new software and was eager to try it out.

Two Sundays before the event, everyone sat eagerly awaiting Hunter's latest installment. As the sanctuary darkened, sounds of helicopters and machine guns blasted from the speakers. A collage of battered war zone images flashed across the screen. The camera cut to dirty, barefoot children crying and holding up empty bowls. This image morphed into a hospital emergency room where doctors and nurses unsuccessfully try to save a patient. A heavy metal soundtrack played loudly over a narrator's words, which the audience strained to hear. A montage of patriotic images filled the screen—the President giving a speech, voters going to the polls, flags waving. The clip ended with the words, "see you at the pole" in tiny calligraphy at the bottom of the screen.

One by one, the audience turned to each other and asked, "Are we supposed to vote?"

Hunter may have thought his video a great artistic work, but the message somehow got lost in all the special effects and images. While we may be creating our own works of art in the church, we must never lose sight of the message we are trying to convey. Sometimes "simple" gets the message across more effectively than "fancy."

Lord of all, help me to remember the message is more important than the messenger. I don't want people to see me in my work, but to see you. May your truth be evident in whatever I do for you.

Stepping Out of Your Comfort Zone

The LORD turned to him and said, "Go in the strength you have and save Israel out of Midian's hand. Am I not sending you?" "But Lord," Gideon asked, "how can I save Israel? My clan is the weakest in Manasseh, and I am the least in my family."

Judges 6:14–15

Bonus Reading: Judges 6:36–40; Acts 8:26–40

Heidi put down the telephone. "Another no," she sighed. Heidi had been calling her friends asking if any of them would accompany her to help out at the rescue mission thrift store once a month.

"It's too far away," said one.

"I'm scared of the people who frequent places like that," said another.

"I'm involved in enough ministries already," said the last.

Lord, do you really want me to serve you at the mission thrift store? Heidi prayed. Her pastor had announced the need for volunteers last Sunday. Anyone interested was to see him. So far, only Heidi had responded.

Heidi began to think about all the excuses her friends gave her. *Are they true for me too? Does God truly want me to go?* she wondered. She stood up and took her Bible from the shelf above her desk. She looked up the story of Gideon putting out the fleece to determine if God really wanted him to save Israel. Gideon gave God excuses for not following his call. *I don't want to test God by "putting out a fleece,"* she thought.

Heidi then turned to the story of Philip leaving his successful preaching ministry in Samaria to meet the Ethiopian eunuch on the desert road. Philip could have thought, *I've been preaching to hundreds and baptizing many. Why should I go all that way just to speak to one man?* As Heidi kept reading she realized that after the Ethiopian received Christ, he brought Christianity back to his own country and continued the spread of the gospel.

Heidi almost gasped as she realized how this story applied to her. Philip went alone to a faraway place to share God's love with one man. How much more could she serve God by "stepping out of her comfort zone" and reaching out to someone with whom she would normally not have contact? Who knows how her life could affect one person who in turn could influence many for God?

Heidi picked up the phone and called her pastor. "Can you give me directions to the rescue mission?" she asked.

Heidi obeyed God's leading to join a ministry even when none of her friends wanted to. Is God urging you to serve him in a new area? Are you giving him excuses or obeying his call?

Heavenly Father, I know you want me to join this ministry despite all the reasons against it. Give me the courage to follow you, even if others don't.

Work It Out

If your brother sins against you, go and show him his fault, just between the two of you. If he listens to you, you have won your brother over.

Matthew 18:15

Bonus Reading: Matthew 18:15–17, Psalm 133:1

Tonia and Marie help out at the soup kitchen downtown. They also attend the same youth group at church. Marie was elected vice president of the club, with Tonia coming in a close second. Tonia accused Marie of being nice to people just so they would vote for her. Now both girls are not speaking to each other.

At the soup kitchen, the girls serve food cafeteria style. They stand next to each other as the clientele bring trays up to be filled at the kitchen window. The girls avoid making eye contact with each other and leave plenty of space between the two of them. They move stiffly and fill the trays more noisily and less neatly than they usually do.

Marie accidentally drops a ladle and splatters Tonia's shoes with spaghetti sauce. "Now you've done it!" Tonia seethes. "Gimme that towel." She points to the towel next to Marie.

"Get it yourself!" Marie retorts as she picks up the ladle and moves toward the sink at the back of the kitchen.

A grizzled old man stands at the window with a knowing look on his face. "Seems you two need to get by yourself and work somethin' out."

Tonia bends down to wipe the sauce off her shoes. She rises and whispers, "You have no idea what she did to me." She hurries off to throw the towel in the wash bin.

Marie returns with a clean ladle. The man asks, "What d'ya do to her?"

"I didn't do anything to her. She did something to me," Marie says.

Tonia returns and the two fill the man's plate. As he is about to leave he remarks, "Doesn't the Bible say somethin' about Christians walkin' together in unity? Think about it."

The two continue to fill plates in silence. At the end, they both speak at once.

"You first," Marie offers.

"No, you go ahead," Tonia replies.

"Let's go somewhere where we can talk," Marie says.

The two head to the storage room near the kitchen and take the first steps toward reconciliation.

When members of a team are having relational conflict, it not only affects them, it affects their performance on the team and those to whom they minister. Marie and Tonia became sloppy in their job and were a poor testimony to the soup kitchen clientele. Working together in unity is a strong statement to the world of Christ's love and transforming power.

Dear God, I know what the Bible says about resolving conflict with fellow Christians, but it is so hard to obey. I don't want to admit my feelings have been hurt. I don't want people to know I am vulnerable. Please give me the courage to make things right.

A Valuable Talent

Here is a boy with five small barley loaves and two small fish, but how far will they go among so many?

John 6:9

Bonus Reading: 2 Kings 4:42–44

As Ray was jogging out the door of the shopping mall, a stranger stopped him. "Do you speak Cantonese?" he asked.

"Yes . . ." Ray replied suspiciously.

"There's an Asian man upstairs who says he speaks Cantonese and he's lost," the stranger explained. "Can you go up there and help him?"

Excuse after excuse flashed through Ray's mind. *Is there really a man upstairs or is this a trick? Just because I look Chinese this guy thinks I speak Cantonese. I have to get home for dinner. I have to wrap this present I just bought.* Sighing, Ray turned around and stepped onto the escalator. He wondered if he was doing the right thing. At the top of the escalator, he spied an old Chinese man sitting down on a bench and a Caucasian man standing next to him.

"What seems to be the trouble?" Ray asked the second stranger.

"This man doesn't know where his family is and I can't help him because he doesn't speak much English. Can you try speaking to him in Cantonese?"

Ray knelt down next to the older gentleman and began talking in Cantonese. After a brief conversation, the man pulled out a wallet with a list of phone numbers inside. He handed the list to Ray.

"That's great!" the second man's face lit up as he pulled out a cell phone. "I could never have gotten him to do that. Now we can call someone to come get him."

"I guess knowing a second language comes in handy sometimes," Ray said.

"But the key is that you were willing to use it to help someone else," the man replied as he punched in the number.

The old man's daughter came to pick him up. "Thank you for helping my father. This is not the first time he has wandered off without telling anyone. We are very grateful."

Ray could have ignored the plea for help as he rushed out of the mall. But instead he took the time to use a skill that he may not have thought of as valuable. Just like the little boy who gave up his meager lunch to the Master, you may not think you have much to offer God, but he can use anyone who is willing to follow his leading.

Heavenly Father, I don't know how you want to use me today, but I pray that I will not pass up any opportunity you lay before me to do good.

Patience, Dear

Everyone should be quick to listen, slow to speak and slow to become angry, for man's anger does not bring about the righteous life that God desires.

James 1:19–20

Bonus Reading: James 3:3–6

Bernard and Sonja organized a citywide marriage conference at a large community center. One hundred fifty couples from various churches attended the two-day event. However, Bernard and Sonja didn't have a chance to listen to the speaker because they had many details to sort out. They closed the doors behind them as they stepped out into the foyer.

"Sonja, shouldn't the helpers be here by now? Have you called Carrie?"

"I thought you were going to contact her!"

"No, you said you were."

Sonja rolled her eyes. "I'll call her now." She dialed the number. "Carrie, what time are you all coming to set up lunch?" she asked. "Eleven thirty? That only gives you a half hour. Are you sure that's enough time?" Sonja shot an alarmed look at Bernard. "No, lunch is at twelve, not twelve thirty. Just get your people here as fast as you can." She hung up and growled between her teeth.

"Maybe the speaker will run late," Bernard said hopefully.

"Maybe if you told Carrie the change in schedule, she would be here by now," Sonja snapped.

"Let's not argue about it. We still have to set up the book table."

Bernard opened a box and began taking out stacks of books. Sonja carefully propped one copy of each book in front of its stack. She shook her head and sighed as Bernard accidentally knocked some books over. "We should have done this before everyone got here so they could browse early," she said as they picked up the fallen books.

"We couldn't help it that the baby-sitter came late. Let's just chill out."

"Don't tell me to chill . . ." Sonja began. She put the books down. "I'm sorry. I shouldn't yell at you."

"No problem. I'm used to it," Bernard grinned and gave Sonja a hug. "Everything will turn out fine."

Sonja needed to exercise more patience with her spouse. In times of stress, it is easy to argue and place the blame on other people, justly or unjustly. No one and nothing is perfect and we have to accept people and situations as they are. Getting angry doesn't help. It only adds more fuel to the fire.

Patient Father, I confess I'm not always tolerant of others. I get angry easily. Help me to be more patient and loving toward those around me, especially when I'm under pressure.

Is Someone Jealous of You?

Joseph had a dream, and when he told it to his brothers, they hated him all the more.

Genesis 37:5

Bonus Reading: Genesis 37:3–11

Brock and Dwight played basketball in the church gym every Thursday night. The youth pastor started this sports ministry to reach young men who would not normally attend church on Sundays. Both high schoolers received Christ as a result of attending this event.

The teenagers loved the game and competed hard. Tonight, Brock dribbled his way down the court, slam-dunked, and held onto the rim. Dwight stood by with a scowl on his face.

The youth pastor called Brock over to the sideline. "Brock, I need to tell you something."

"What is it, man? You can be straight with me," Brock panted.

"I think Dwight might be jealous of you."

"No way! What makes you say that?"

"You always get chosen first, then he's second. You score more points than him. And by the look on his face when you slam-dunked, it was pretty obvious."

"What can I do about it? I can't make myself play bad. And I can't control how he feels."

"You might try not rubbing in his face the fact that you're a better player than him."

"Have I been doing that?" Brock said incredulously.

"When you dribble between your legs all the time and do those other fancy moves, it looks like you're showing off."

Brock whistled. "I never thought of that. I just like doing what I see the pros do. But I guess it's like what you said the other day. We shouldn't do stuff to make our brother stumble."

"You get the idea. Now go back and play a great game."

Brock agreed not to show off to ease Dwight's jealousy. In the Bible, Joseph's brothers envied him when his father gave him the multi-colored coat. When he told his brothers the dream that someday he would rule over them, they became more jealous. Joseph could have chosen not to say anything. Revealing the dream opened the door to more hostility from his brothers.

Lord, I know someone who is jealous of me. Help me to avoid doing anything to make him more jealous. Deal with his heart—help him to see how valuable he is to you.

Music That Communicates

> Even in the case of lifeless things that make sounds, such as the flute or harp, how will anyone know what tune is being played unless there is a distinction in the notes? Again, if the trumpet does not sound a clear call, who will get ready for battle? So it is with you. Unless you speak intelligible words with your tongue, how will anyone know what you are saying? You will just be speaking into the air.
>
> 1 Corinthians 14:7–9

Bonus Reading: 1 Corinthians 14:6–12

Kaydie was visiting church for the first time. She sat down with her friend Rita, who had invited her. Four people stood before microphones at the front of the auditorium. Above their heads a movie screen came down and flashed words to a song. The musicians began playing and the four people began singing. Everyone stood up, so Kaydie rose too. She looked around and noticed other people were singing with the people in front. She began singing too. Although she didn't know the song, she easily caught on.

After a few more tunes, everyone sat down and a woman stepped up to the mike to sing a solo. Kaydie thought it strange that this woman stood like a statue with her hands at her sides, looking straight ahead, with no expression on her face. Kaydie tried to listen to the lyrics, but couldn't concentrate. The woman sang beautifully, but Kaydie couldn't remember a word she said.

The woman sat down and the group of four came up again. Kaydie noticed now that when this group sang, they smiled, made eye contact with the audience, and moved their hands and heads in a natural way. The expressions on their faces matched the words they were singing. Kaydie wiped a tear from her eye as she thought about the message of the song.

After the last prayer, Rita asked Kaydie, "How did you like the service?"

Kaydie replied, "It was different. I liked the singing, especially of the—what do you call it—the worship team? It was really moving."

"I'm glad you liked it," Rita said. "I hope you'll have time to come back again."

When we communicate God's message through song, do we connect with our audience? Can they understand what we are singing about? Do our facial expressions and body language match the words we are saying? Do we look at the congregation as we sing? People who are new to church may have only secular examples of singers to compare us to. If we look like robots when we sing, they may not think Christianity is worth exploring. But if we show that Christ makes a difference in our lives through our singing, they may be more open to him.

Holy Singer, may I strive to make the words of Christian songs real in my life. May I express the message effectively in a way that connects with people. Help me communicate your Word to touch lives.

I Don't Feel like Forgiving

Bear with each other and forgive whatever grievances you may have against one another. Forgive as the Lord forgave you.

Colossians 3:13

Bonus Reading: Luke 15:25–32

Arielle and Nadine work in the puppet ministry. Once a month, they act out Bible stories for children's church. The two women make up their own dialogue. This Sunday, they performed a story entitled "Daniel in the Boxing Ring."

After the children left, the Sunday school superintendent marched up to them. "What did you think you were doing? That's *not* how the story goes. You'll confuse the kids. Next time, look it up in the Bible and do it right!" he snapped as he stormed out of the room.

The two wide-eyed women stared at each other with mouths agape. "I can't believe he said that to us," Arielle whispered.

"Who does he think he is yelling at us like that? We didn't do anything wrong!" Nadine exclaimed.

"I thought our interpretation stuck with the meaning of the story. These older kids have heard it a million times and they'd be bored stiff if we did it the 'regular way.' They know what parts are from the Bible and which are not," Arielle said quietly.

"He can have his own opinion, but he shouldn't have spoken to us in that tone of voice." Nadine put her puppet in her bag. "His attitude makes me mad."

"Yes, he should be more sensitive to people's feelings. What he said really hurt," said Arielle.

The two women continued to pack away their equipment, silently stewing. Finally Arielle spoke. "You know what? Maybe he had a bad morning. Maybe he's not feeling well. I need to forgive him so *I* don't keep feeling bad. I don't want to take out my anger on anyone like he did on us."

"I know you're right. But I don't feel very forgiving right now. Will you pray for me?" Nadine asked.

"Let's pray right now."

When someone hurts our feelings with disparaging words, it is normal to feel defensive or angry. But if we do not let go of these negative emotions, they will turn into bitterness. Forgiving from our hearts makes us feel better. We can't control how others act toward us, but we can control our own actions.

Comforter, I have been hurt very badly by another's words. Give me the grace to forgive that person even if he or she doesn't apologize.

Are You Overworked?

A man can do nothing better than to eat and drink and find satisfaction in his work. This too, I see, is from the hand of God, for without him, who can eat or find enjoyment?

Ecclesiastes 2:24–25

Bonus Reading: Ecclesiastes 2:22–26

Trevor served God in many areas. A carpet layer by trade, he cheerfully used his professional skills to recarpet the church hallways on Tuesday. He loved tinkering with cars, so on Wednesday, he changed the oil in the church van. He chaperoned his son's youth group at the ice rink on Friday. Active in the mens fellowship and a natural organizer, he helped put together a mens prayer breakfast on Saturday. And finally, as a deacon, he headed up the Clergy Appreciation Service on Sunday night and even emceed the event. The congregation loved his humorous stories about each of the pastors.

On Monday morning, however, he yelled at his assistant for arriving three minutes late. When the church van driver called later that evening and said the vehicle was making a funny noise, he told him to take it to a garage and bill the church. Later that week he complained to his wife that he would never again chaperone the youth group. When his friend in the mens fellowship asked him to help plan the mens retreat, he flatly refused. And at the next deacons meeting, he was strangely silent.

Was Trevor losing his commitment to the church? No! He was just plain burnt out. He acted uncharacteristically irritable toward his helper. He normally liked working on cars, but he didn't love it when the van driver called. He usually enjoyed handling large projects, but refused to participate in planning the retreat. And for Trevor to be silent anywhere, let alone a deacons meeting, was absolutely unheard of.

Do you feel overworked in your volunteer duties? There will be crunch times when many church events occur within a short period of time. Try to spread out your commitments so that you can spend enough time on all of them without feeling overburdened. Learn to say "no" graciously.

Lord of all, I want to serve you to the best of my abilities. Thank you for giving me different talents. Help me to be wise in using them so that I don't burn out. Give me the strength to persevere through busy seasons.

A Teachable Spirit

Flog a mocker, and the simple will learn prudence;
rebuke a discerning man, and he will gain knowledge.

Proverbs 19:25

Bonus Reading: Proverbs 9:7–10

The church parking lot was transformed into a winter wonderland for the annual Holiday Craft Fair. Christmas music played quietly behind the chatter of buyers and sellers. Annika's booth resembled a formal dining room. She had set out a long folding table covered with a red tablecloth showcasing her embroidered table runners, placemats, and napkins. Beside it, an artificial tree displayed ornaments made from Styrofoam balls, ribbons, and sequins. A beautiful hand-quilted tree skirt adorned the bottom.

She spied her neighbor Bess browsing at the booth across the way. She waved Bess over.

"So glad you could make it to the craft fair," Annika said.

"Wouldn't miss it for the world," Bess said as she studied Annika's wares. "What a lovely setup you have here," she commented. She turned over the price tag of one of the ornaments. She raised her eyebrows.

"Is anything the matter?" Annika asked.

"Um, have you checked what other people are selling their ornaments for?"

"No, I've been too busy setting up my booth to look around."

Bess shifted uncomfortably. "These ornaments are priced much higher than any of the other ones I've seen."

Annika folded her arms. "I put a lot of work into those ornaments. My fingers are sore from pushing all those stick pins in for the sequins."

"I'm sure you spent a lot of time making these. They are beautiful," Bess began, "but I don't think many people will be willing to pay this high a price."

Annika's eyes fell. She fingered an ornament. "I guess you're right. No one has bought a single item since we began an hour and a half ago."

"Why don't you do this," Bess suggested. "Make a sign that says 'Buy two, get a third one free.' People are always attracted by a sale. Then toward the end of the day, make another sign saying 'All items, half off.' I'm sure you'll sell more that way."

Annika's eyes brightened. "That's a great idea, especially the first part. I hope I won't have much left at the end of the day to have to sell half off. I saw some cardboard near the garbage bins. Maybe I can use some for the signs."

"Stay right there. I'll get it," Bess said as she rushed off to get the cardboard.

At first Annika resisted Bess's constructive criticism. But as she thought about her lack of sales despite the high quality of her work, she realized her neighbor was right. When others criticize you, you don't have to accept everything they say immediately, but think about it and decide how much of it is valid. Then act upon the part you think is true.

Loving Schoolmaster, help me to have a teachable spirit. I value the insight of others. Help me discern what is accurate and what I can learn from it.

I Give Up!

And if anyone gives even a cup of cold water to one of these little
ones because he is my disciple, I tell you the truth, he will certainly
not lose his reward.

Matthew 10:42

Bonus Reading: Esther 4:16

Sean's skateboard skidded to a stop. "You're kidding, right?"

Jace looked up from his seat on the sidewalk. He fiddled with
his board. "No, the youth group really is passing out tracts on Hal-
loween," Jace insisted.

Sean sat down next to Jace. "You mean, instead of going door to
door *getting* candy, we're supposed to go up to each house, *give* the
owners a tract, and *not* take any candy?" Sean repeated.

"That's what I was told," Jace said as he spun the wheels with
his hand.

Sean let out a whistle. "They really expect us to give up the most
fun night in our entire thirteen years just to pass out tracts?"

"We are getting a little old for trick-or-treat," Jace reminded
him.

"I was hoping to get one more year out of it," Sean said.

Jace put down his skateboard and picked up a brown leaf from
the lawn behind him. He crumpled it in his hand. "There's going
to be a party at Chelsea's house afterward. Everyone who passes out
tracts gets to go."

"Can't I just show up at the party?" Sean asked hopefully.

"No."

Sean leaned back and lay on the grass with his hands behind his
head. "What's so special about these tracts?"

Jace turned to look at Sean. "Haven't you ever read one? They
have a little story that tells the gospel. It's a witnessing thing."

"Do we have to talk?" Sean asked nervously.

Jace pivoted his body around. "All you have to do is say something like this: 'Hi, we're from Oakport Creek Church. We don't want any candy, but we'd like to give you this instead.' And you give them the tract."

Sean sat back up. "That sounds pretty easy. I want to witness, but I don't know how to tell someone exactly how to get saved."

"The tract does that. And it gets them interested in God. Maybe they'll get so interested they'll come to church and find out more. It's like we're planting seeds," Jace explained.

"I can do that. I guess giving up trick-or-treating is worth trying to get someone saved," Sean said as he scooped up his skateboard. "Count me in."

Sean was willing to sacrifice something important to him to help others hear the gospel. Queen Esther was willing to give up her life to save her people. How willing are we to give of our time to help others?

Precious Savior, nothing is more important than pleasing you, even if it means giving up something I hold dear for someone else. May I be willing to follow your leading.

I'm Still Mad

Be kind and compassionate to one another, forgiving each other, just as in Christ God forgave you.

Ephesians 4:32

Bonus Reading: Matthew 18:21–35

"Carmen, this is Hazel. Gus has been in a car accident. We're at the hospital. He's got a concussion and lost a lot of blood. Please tell everyone at church to pray for him. Gotta go. Bye."

Carmen shut off the answering machine. "O God, please be with Gus. Make the bleeding stop. Give the doctors wisdom to treat him. Help him to be okay," she quickly prayed aloud. She flew up the stairs and turned on her home computer. *I've got to e-mail the church list. Then I've got to call . . . Oh no, Lois. I don't want to. I'm still mad at her for backing out of helping me with the Mother's Day luncheon. Maybe she won't be home and I can just leave a message. But what if she answers? I don't want to talk to her.*

Carmen sent a message to everyone on the church e-mail list. She picked up the phone and then put it down again. *I can't call Lois. But if I don't, she can't call the next person on the prayer chain and so on. Gus needs all the prayer he can get. I wish everyone had e-mail . . .*

Then the Holy Spirit spoke in her heart. *Do you really think God will hear your prayers if you harbor unforgiveness?*

No, I guess not, Carmen conceded. She bowed her head. *Lord, forgive me for not forgiving Lois. It's really petty of me to hold a grudge when Gus needs my help. Help me to call Lois right now.*

Carmen picked up the phone and pushed the buttons. "Hello, Lois? This is Carmen. I just got a call from Hazel. Gus is in the hospital . . ."

Forgiveness is an act of the will, not an emotion. We can't always control our emotions, but we can control our actions. When Carmen phoned Lois, she showed that she really forgave her.

Forgiving Father, thank you for not holding my sins against me. Help me to forgive others as you have forgiven me, even when I don't feel like it.

Be Creative

Sing to the LORD a new song,
his praise from the ends of the earth.

Isaiah 42:10

Bonus Reading: Revelation 5:9–14

"What are we going to perform for the dinner, guys?" Jerry asked the rest of the praise band.

Tricia, Heath, and Wayne were gathered in Jerry's garage to practice for the church banquet.

"The theme is 'New Beginnings' and we're celebrating the start of the daughter church. I suppose at least one of the songs should have something to do with that," Tricia said as she tuned her guitar.

"I've never heard of a song that talks about a daughter church specifically," Heath added, setting up her keyboard. "I've heard songs about starting over, beginning a new life in Christ, a 'new song in my heart' . . ."

"We have three songs here that have to do with the word 'new' or 'beginning,'" Wayne announced as he looked over their portfolio of music.

Jerry did a drumroll as Wayne read them off. "I like those," Jerry affirmed. The others nodded. Then he added, "But we still need one more."

"Why don't we make up our own, specifically about the daughter church?" Tricia suggested. "Heath, haven't you written some of your own songs before?"

Heath hesitated. "Yeah, but I would need ideas from all of you."

"We could give you lots of ideas," Jerry said excitedly.

The group began throwing out thoughts as Heath scratched busily on a notepad. When she was done, she read aloud her first attempt at a verse:

Like parents with their newborn child,
We thank you, Lord, for her sweet smile.
Your creation, with its growing pains
Is worth the effort with much to gain.

The others looked at each other. "It's a good start," Jerry said encouragingly.

"Yeah, we can keep working on it," Tricia said.

"I like the idea that we're creating this for our own church. It's an original song that can mean a great deal to those listening to it," Wayne said.

Heath closed her notepad. "I'll keep writing at home. But now I think we should practice the other three songs."

The praise band literally created a new song to exalt Christ and praise his name. The church will remember their daughter church every time they hear that song. Has your church reached a historic moment? Perhaps you can write a song about it.

Master Musician, you have blessed our church in so many ways. We want to praise you with our voices and create music to glorify your name. We give our talents over to you.

A Healthy Self

Better one handful with tranquillity
than two handfuls with toil
and chasing after the wind.

Ecclesiastes 4:6

Bonus Reading: 3 John 2

Nolan drove a bus each Sunday morning downtown to pick up kids for Sunday school. This morning he got up at 6:00, drove to the bus yard to check the vehicle, and started his route by 7:30. He arrived at church by 9:00, sleepy and blowing his nose.

"You look terrible, Nolan," his friend Fitz said to him. "Do you have the flu?"

"No, it's just a cold," Nolan replied. The two men entered their Sunday school class.

As the teacher proceeded through the lesson, Nolan began nodding his head. Fitz elbowed him and he sat up with a start. He tried to hide his embarrassment with a tissue, but only attracted more attention as he blew his nose.

After class, Fitz asked, "So did you stay up late last night watching that movie?"

"Yeah. I know what you're going to tell me." Nolan did his best imitation of his mother: "'You should go to bed earlier and take better care of yourself. Don't come to church if you're sick. You'll spread your germs around.'"

Fitz laughed. "I guess I don't need to lecture you. Hope you feel better."

After service, Nolan drove the busload of children home. As he was reaching for another tissue, a car began crossing the intersection directly in front of the bus. Nolan slammed on the brakes. The children were thrown forward, hitting their heads on the seats in front of them. The bus stopped inches from the car. Nolan quickly undid his seat belt and got up to check the children. "Is everyone okay?"

No one was hurt badly. A few had bruises and one boy had scratched his hand on a screw protruding from the seat in front of him. They were all a bit shaken. After making sure the other driver was all right, Nolan resumed his route. He silently thanked God for protection. He felt guilty, though, about the part his cold played in the near-accident. *If I weren't reaching for the tissue, I would have been concentrating on the road better. I would have slowed down more gradually. My reaction time would have been quicker. From now on, I'm going to bed at a decent time on Saturday night and finding a replacement if I'm sick.*

Nolan had to learn a concrete lesson on the importance of taking care of his physical body. We all need to take time for proper rest and care for our bodies especially when we are ill. Not only is physical health important, but spiritual health as well. Do we regularly confess our sins, pray, and read the Bible? Do we meet with other believers for encouragement and fellowship?

Father, I don't always take care of myself physically or spiritually. Help me to do a better job of it.

Grieving the Loss of a Ministry

Then David and all the men with him took hold of their clothes and tore them. They mourned and wept and fasted till evening for Saul and his son Jonathan, and for the army of the LORD and the house of Israel, because they had fallen by the sword.

2 Samuel 1:11–12

Bonus Reading: Nehemiah 1:1–11

"You can't be serious!" Faith cried into the phone.

"I just heard today. They're closing their doors for good." Kaye's voice seemed far away.

"I . . . I can't believe we have to shut down," Faith said in a thick voice. "Thanks for calling."

Faith wiped the tears from her eyes as she hung up. The crisis pregnancy hotline was folding. The organization was unable to pay its bills and could no longer provide help to the women who called in about their unplanned babies.

Faith had a passion for the unborn. She herself had decided not to have an abortion after calling the hotline. After her baby was born, she wanted to help other women come to the same decision she had and volunteered to answer the phones twice a week.

As a prerequisite to answering the calls, Faith took a grief counseling course in case women who had had an abortion called. In that course she learned that besides death, other life crises can cause grief such as loss of a job, freedom, or lifestyle. In her case, she just lost her ministry.

Faith knew she had to take the time to grieve. She met with her fellow volunteers and they cried together. But they didn't wallow in self-pity. They discussed other ideas on how to help pregnant women. They turned their grief into action.

Have you ever lost a ministry? Has your church ever decided to stop supporting your ministry? For whatever reasons the loss occurred, it is a real crisis that you must deal with. Nehemiah mourned the deplorable conditions of Jerusalem, but then he got up and did something about them. In the same way, when we lose a ministry, we need to move on and think of other ways to serve God.

Comforter, you know how much my ministry meant to me. You know how I loved the people and the cause. I feel rotten right now. If ever I needed your comfort, I need it now. Help me to get over the loss and go on serving you in other areas.

Cooperate instead of Compete

All the believers were one in heart and mind. No one claimed that any of his possessions was his own, but they shared everything they had.

Acts 4:32

Bonus Reading: Acts 4:32–37

"What a beautiful cake, Marsha!" Eleanor said with a hint of sarcasm. Marsha was putting on the finishing touches to her tea party cake when Eleanor "accidentally" bumped into the cake table. "Oh, I'm so sorry!" Eleanor quickly said as Marsha dropped a sugar leaf.

Marsha glared at Eleanor. "I'm sure you are." As Eleanor walked back to her own cake, Marsha whispered to a friend. "She did that on purpose. She doesn't want anyone to buy my cake before someone buys hers. If you ask me, that poor excuse for an apple streusel cake will sit there all afternoon."

Both Eleanor and Marsha baked delicious desserts. Each year at the church bake sale they tried to outdo each other in who could sell her wares first and whose was the most elaborate. What started out as a friendly competition turned into an all-out war. That year, neither of their cakes sold because no one wanted to upset either woman.

Realizing the error of their ways, both women declared a truce. They apologized to each other and recognized that their attitudes were not glorifying to God or helping their church. This year they decided to cooperate instead of compete. They each made several batches of different cookies and combined them to fill gift baskets. These sold like hotcakes and everyone marveled at how relaxing the bake sale seemed this year.

Friendly competition can stir up creativity, but when it gets out of hand, it can lead to hurt feelings and bad testimonies. The early Christians cooperated with each other and shared what they had with their brothers and sisters. In the same way, we need to show Christ's love to one another and not let selfishness or pride become a stumbling block to younger believers or non-Christians.

Dear Lord, there are others in my church who have similar talents to mine. Help us to use these abilities for your glory and not for our own. Let us endeavor to cooperate with one another and not compete.

Ready, Set—Go!

> In the second month of the second year after their arrival at the house of God in Jerusalem, Zerubbabel son of Shealtiel, Jeshua son of Jozadak and the rest of their brothers (the priests and the Levites and all who had returned from the captivity to Jerusalem) began the work, appointing Levites twenty years of age and older to supervise the building of the house of the LORD.
>
> Ezra 3:8

Bonus Reading: Ezra 3:8–13

Lionel pulled into the church parking lot. He whistled in amazement to see several cars already there. *I thought* I *was early,* he said to himself. As head trustee and coordinator of the annual work day in May, Lionel had begun thinking about this year's event soon after last year's was over. Within the last five months, he met several times with the other trustees to pray and explain his vision, goals, and methods and gain their feedback to make the day a success.

Lionel envisioned getting the whole church involved in caring for the physical property God had given them. From the trustees' discussion, they identified and prioritized several areas that needed attention, including repainting the sanctuary, trimming the landscaping, and clearing out junk from storage areas. They decided to target the youth groups, adult home teams, and Sunday school classes to sign up large groups of volunteers.

Lionel began announcing the event to the church via e-mail at the beginning of the year. He contacted leaders of the various church ministries to garner their support of the project. He announced what specific tasks they would tackle through "ads" in the bulletin, newsletter, and bulletin boards. One month before the event, he began asking parishioners to sign up so the trustees could estimate how much work could be done and how much food would be needed.

Individual trustees headed up specific areas. They asked volunteers to bring some of their own equipment. A committee made preparations for lunch and snacks to feed the hundreds of volunteers they expected.

Although Lionel had done all he could humanly do to get ready for this day, he still had butterflies. *What if it rains? What if those who signed up don't show? What if the equipment breaks down?* As he glanced at the blue sky and eyed more cars arriving, he knew in his head the results were in God's hands, but his heart told him to pray. As the people gathered around him, Lionel asked God's blessings on the day.

No matter what ministry you are involved with, proper preparation is always necessary. Zerubbabel and the exiles took nine months preparing to build the temple. Lionel and his trustees planned many months for the work day. Although we give God the ultimate glory for any success, he expects us to prepare as much as possible.

Dear God, I want to serve you in a certain area, but I need proper preparation. Help me to gain the experience I need to do a good job.

Nursery Blues

Obey your leaders and submit to their authority. They keep watch over you as men who must give an account. Obey them so that their work will be a joy, not a burden, for that would be of no advantage to you.

Hebrews 13:17

Bonus Reading: 1 Thessalonians 5:12–13

Penny lifted the eight-month-old from her mother's arms. "Hello, Amber," she cooed. "Ready to see your friends?" Penny baby-sat in the church nursery. As a mother of twins, she had plenty of experience with babies.

Joyce, the woman in charge of the nursery, took the baby's diaper bag. "Feed her at 10:30, change her at 11:30, right?" The mother smiled and nodded, then quickly departed before her baby noticed she was gone.

Joyce slipped the bottle of formula out of the bag and placed it in the refrigerator. An experienced mother herself, she had worked hard to make the nursery a safe and inviting place to welcome the infants during church services.

At 10:30, Penny took Amber's bottle from the fridge. She started placing it in the microwave oven to warm up.

"Penny, please use the bottle warmer next to the sink. The microwave doesn't heat the formula evenly, and it may become too hot for Amber to drink," Joyce warned.

"I do this all the time at home," Penny countered. "I just swish the bottle around a few times to mix it up."

"I'd rather you put it in the warmer," Joyce reiterated.

Penny rolled her eyes and put the bottle in the warmer.

At 11:30, Penny changed Amber. She placed her down on the floor and reached for the next baby.

"Penny, can you wash your hands before changing the next one?" Joyce asked.

112

"I always change both twins before I wash my hands. It saves time."

"These babies are from different families. I think the parents would appreciate the extra precaution not to spread germs," Joyce said.

Penny plopped the baby down and spun around toward the sink.

At 12:00 the parents came to pick up their children. Amber's mother said, "Thank you for taking care of my baby. I know she's in good hands when I leave her here."

"We try our best," Joyce smiled.

Penny obeyed Joyce, but did it grudgingly. How much easier Joyce's job would be if Penny obeyed cheerfully without excuses or back talk! We must remember that those in authority are accountable to God. Our responsibility is to obey them wholeheartedly, even if we have differences of opinion.

Righteous Ruler, help me to obey my leaders with a good attitude. You have placed them there to guide us. Give me a humble spirit and a willing heart.

Come Join Us!

Moses said to the whole Israelite community . . . "All who are skilled among you are to come and make everything the LORD has commanded."

Exodus 35:4, 10

Bonus Reading: Exodus 35:4–19

Neal had a great idea. He wanted to network all the church's computers together so the people who use them could share printers, communicate with one another, and access the Internet easier. Not a talkative person, he was reluctant to express his thoughts. However, he knew God was gently nudging him toward action. He finally brought his idea to the church leaders and they approved. Now all he had to do was get several others to help him and they could finish the job in one day.

Neal e-mailed the whole church to find out who was interested and when they were available. He set a date and ten "computer whizzes" showed up. That Saturday morning, they finished the job in record time. They all went out to lunch at the local fast-food restaurant.

The men pushed several tables together and sat down with their trays of food. Neal remarked, "The work sure went fast. I can't believe we're already done."

Howard reached for a french fry and said, "Yeah, I guess it helps to have ten guys doing it at once. It was fun."

"We should do something like this again," Terry added.

"Maybe we could combine all the databases of the different church ministries into one database?" Neal suggested. "That way, the ministries can share information."

"That's a great idea," Howard said. The others nodded as they downed their lunches.

114

"It would take just one guy to be in charge and several to help him," Terry remarked.

"Neal's our man!" Howard said as he clapped him on the back. The others cheered.

Neal blushed. He managed to say, "If you guys are willing, I'll see if we can get approval." The others looked at each other and expressed their agreement.

The guys threw out other ideas as they finished their lunch. As they rose to dispose of their trash, Neal said, "I think we may have started a new ministry."

Neal thought of a way to help the church. Do you desire to serve God in a way that requires other people's assistance? Neal overcame his shyness and took the first step by talking to someone about it. Then he followed through and asked others for their involvement.

Master, I wish to serve you in a certain area. I'm afraid, though, to ask the leaders about it. Give me the courage to speak and to get others involved.

Mumble Grumble

Do everything without complaining or arguing.

Philippians 2:14

Bonus Reading: Exodus 15:22–25

Quincy, Graham, and Mariana embarked on their first short-term missions trip to China. Before leaving, the whole group had to pass a training program where they learned of the primitive living conditions existing in China. When they arrived in Shanghai, however, they marveled at how modern the city appeared. But their destination lay south of the big city in a small rural village. Here, they planned to teach English to high school students and quietly respond to opportunities to share the gospel.

At the dormitory, which would be their home for the next three weeks, straw mats on the floor served as their beds. Cold showers greeted them in the morning and meager meals wafted unfamiliar aromas.

At breakfast, Quincy said, "I could hardly sleep a wink last night. The crickets kept chirping and that mat was hard as a rock. I've camped in better conditions than this before."

Graham said, "Me too. That cold shower this morning was the shortest I've ever taken. I'm still freezing."

Mariana looked at her plate of food. "What is this green thing? It looks like one of your crickets, Quincy!" She shoved the plate away.

"Why did we ever sign up for this trip? I wanna go home!" Graham said.

Other short-termers looked their way. They began complaining too and pretty soon the whole room filled with murmuring. The head missionary walked in.

"What's all this complaining I hear?" he asked. "You're here for a very special purpose—to help these kids. Remember our friend from Tarsus? His very life was in danger countless times, yet he never complained. He was content with whatever state he was in."

The group hung their heads. One by one they picked up their utensils and began to eat. Mariana cut off a piece of her food and put it in her mouth. She chewed slowly. After swallowing, she said, "Not bad for a cricket."

Grumbling and complaining are contagious. They can spread more quickly than a virus. The Israelites were constantly griping and spent forty years in the wilderness for that and other sins. Complaining will kill teamwork and squelch team spirit.

Gracious Giver, forgive me for grumbling. I need to remember your blessings in times when I feel like complaining. Help me contribute to team spirit rather than undermine it.

Red Tape *Can* Work for You

> The next day, since the commander wanted to find out exactly why Paul was being accused by the Jews, he released him and ordered the chief priests and all the Sanhedrin to assemble. Then he brought Paul and had him stand before them. . . . Five days later the high priest Ananias went down to Caesarea with some of the elders and a lawyer named Tertullus, and they brought their charges against Paul before the governor.
>
> Acts 22:30; 24:1

Bonus Reading: Acts 25:12, 23; 27:1

Saralyn loved selling and browsing at the local flea market. One day as she was walking through the market, she had an idea. *The church needs to repair the sanctuary. Why not host a gigantic yard sale to raise the money? People can clean out their closets, help the church, and assist poor people who can't afford to shop at regular stores. The leftovers can be donated to various thrift charities that also minister to the down-and-out.*

Saralyn talked to some of her friends who agreed to help out. One reminded her that she needed to speak with the pastor before she went any further. When she asked the pastor, he promised to take the idea to the church council. Saralyn had to wait one month before the council finally approved. They also added two more people to Saralyn's informal committee. She met again with the core group, set a date, and outlined a plan.

The following Sunday, Saralyn bumped into the church secretary after service. "Gina, how do I get reimbursed for placing a yard sale ad in the newspaper?"

Gina replied, "You have to fill out a check request form, attach a receipt, get it approved by a deacon, and turn it in to the treasurer."

"That's a lot of steps to go through," Saralyn remarked. As Gina turned to leave, Saralyn added, "I'm in charge of setup. Can I just take the tables and chairs from the storage room?"

"Oh no, you have to fill out a request to the custodial staff, tell them how many of what you need, the date you need them, and who is going to pick them up and put them away," the secretary said. "And you have to get it approved by a deacon too."

Saralyn raised her eyebrows. "You mean I can't just ask the custodian for a key?"

Gina shook her head.

"There sure is a lot of red tape," Saralyn sighed.

"It's necessary because our church is so large. Your requests have to be down on paper so they don't get forgotten. Because there are so many needs, the leaders have to prioritize them for the staff so they don't get overwhelmed." Gina patted Saralyn on the arm. "You just have to know the system. Then it gets easier. Don't worry, it'll be worth the trouble in the long run."

"I sure hope so. Thanks for the info," Saralyn said as Gina walked off.

Saralyn began to wonder if the yard sale would be worth all the trouble she had to go through. Dealing with bureaucracy can sometimes be exasperating. But being familiar with the process of how work gets done at your church will save time and reduce frustration. Paul was no stranger to government administration. He had to defend himself before the Sanhedrin, governors Felix and Festus, and King Agrippa before finally sailing to Rome. In the process, he preached the gospel to hundreds of people who would have never heard him had he gone straight to Rome.

Heavenly Father, I really want to serve you, but the bureaucracy I must overcome is monumental. I'm so frustrated. Give me patience, knowledge, and wisdom to deal with it so I can move forward.

A Volunteering Professional

Each one should use whatever gift he has received to serve others,
faithfully administering God's grace in its various forms.

1 Peter 4:10

Bonus Reading: Galatians 5:13

Alex is a successful medical practitioner in his hometown. "Dr. Al," as everyone knows him, goes on a medical missions trip every summer to South America, where he volunteers in a jungle hospital for two weeks. Back home, he works without pay in the downtown free clinic every Tuesday helping the poor and homeless get medical attention.

Alex is meeting a fellow doctor from his church at a local coffee shop before work.

"How would you like to go to an exotic location for your next vacation?" Dr. Al asks.

Dr. Baldwin peers at Alex above the top of his cup. He puts the cup down. "Okay, I'll bite. What did you have in mind?"

"How about Brazil?"

Dr. Baldwin scowls. "You're not trying to get me to go on that medical missions trip, are you?"

"Why not? You said you wanted to do something different this year."

"It didn't include working. Especially for free," Dr. Baldwin said as he took another sip.

Alex put his cup down. "It's a very fulfilling experience. You can really see God's hand at work."

"How so?"

"The people down there have nothing compared to us. Conditions are very primitive. But the clinic brings a ray of hope to them. They see these foreign doctors come in and are impressed that we would choose to volunteer our time with them. It opens the door for the gospel. Many become curious about our beliefs and ask questions. When we show them God's love, they respond. Many are healed not just physically at the clinic, but spiritually as well."

Dr. Baldwin sighed. "I'd have to think about it."

"We could really use a pediatrician like you. So many children come in needing medical attention. And their hearts are wide open."

Dr. Baldwin rubbed his forehead. "If you have a brochure or something, I'll take a look at it."

"Sure, I can give it to you tomorrow. We're holding an information session this Sunday after church. Why don't you stop by and hear what the others have to say about it."

"I'll come, but no promises," Dr. Baldwin replied.

"You won't regret it."

Does your church need your professional skills? Maybe you are not a health care provider, but a teacher, architect, plumber, or electrician. Whatever your profession, be willing to use all your abilities for God.

Lord, thank you for my profession. Not only do I earn my living from it to support my family, but I dedicate it and all my skills to you. May I take opportunities to use my job skills to advance your kingdom.

I'm Gonna Let It Shine

Let your light shine before men, that they may see your good deeds and praise your Father in heaven.

Matthew 5:16

Bonus Reading: Matthew 5:13–16

Iris and her son set out for the beach—not for a summer's day lazing by the sea, but to join others in their community to take care of their environment. On this windy autumn day, dozens of families, armed with garbage bags, gloves, and pokers walked the sands picking up trash.

"Why are we doing this, Mommy?" five-year-old Corey asked.

"We want to take care of God's world. We also want to show others we care about the place we live in," Iris explained.

"Isn't it enough that we clean up our house?" Corey asked.

"Well, we should keep our homes clean, but we also want to meet others in our area. Volunteering is a good way to do just that," Iris replied.

"Why do we want to meet other people? Don't we know enough at school and church?"

"Most of the people at church and some of the people at your Christian school already know Jesus Christ. We want to introduce others to Jesus who don't know him," Iris said.

As they continued their way down the beach, they met another family picking up garbage. Iris introduced herself and Corey.

"My name's Madeline," a woman in her thirties said. "And this is my son Irving."

The two women struck up a conversation while they and the boys filled their bags. At noon, all the families gathered for a tailgate party in the parking lot.

"Be sure to pick up all your trash," the organizer announced at the end of the meal. Everyone laughed.

Iris turned to Madeline. "It was sure nice meeting you today. Hope to see you again."

"I enjoyed meeting you too. Maybe someday I'll come and visit the church you were telling me about," Madeline said.

The two women exchanged phone numbers. Corey waved goodbye to Irving. "Can you come to Sunday school? We have lots of fun there."

"Can I go, Mom?" Irving asked.

"We'll see," Madeline replied.

As Iris opened the car door for Corey, he said, "I thought today was going to be boring, but I really had fun."

"I'm glad you did, son. Working for Jesus gives me a good feeling inside too."

Becoming friends with non-Christians is often the first step toward getting them interested in spiritual matters. Volunteering in the community is one way to meet new people. Does your life attract others to God? Showing you care about your neighborhood helps others see Christ in you.

Dear God, help me to be a good testimony to my community. May my life draw others to Christ and not repel them.

Find Us Faithful

Well done, good and faithful servant! You have been faithful with a few things; I will put you in charge of many things. Come and share your master's happiness!

Matthew 25:23

Bonus Reading: Matthew 25:14–30

On Cecil's funeral day, the chapel overflowed with his friends and relatives. Set among the flowers, a table displayed a waffle iron, wooden airplane, and a carburetor. Cecil was dressed in a tattered brown suit and held a hammer in his hands. The preacher stood to give the eulogy.

"Relatives and friends, we are gathered here to honor Cecil's life. Some might think it strange to decorate a funeral home with an appliance, toy, and car part, but these are just representative of the many objects Cecil fixed in his lifetime. He wasn't rich financially and never finished high school, but served God with the talents given him. This is the kind of life we honor today . . ."

After the eulogy, mourners stood up one by one and shared stories of how Cecil impacted their lives. One woman said, "Cecil always greeted me with a smile. I was amazed how he could be so chipper after waking up at 5:30 every Sunday morning to open the church by 7:00."

She sat down and a man rose. "Cecil was a student in my adult Sunday school class. I appreciated the fact he tried to participate in discussions, even if he didn't always get the correct answers."

He sat down as another woman stood slowly. "Just last week, I asked Cecil to come to my home and fix my toilet," she shared. "The water kept running after it was flushed and wouldn't stop. Cecil looked at me and said, 'What? You don't want a singing toilet?'"

The crowd chuckled and the woman sat down. The preacher walked to the podium. "I'm sure Cecil is in heaven right now shining the pearly gates. He faithfully served God every day of his life and is enjoying the happiness of his Master."

When you stand before God, will he be able to say, "Well done, good and faithful servant?" Good works won't earn you a place in heaven, but if you have put your faith in Christ, you will want to do good works. Cecil served God till the end of his life. What have you been doing lately for the Lord?

Master, thank you for the abilities you have given me. Lately, I haven't been using them for you. Renew in me a servant's heart and use me for your glory.

Don't Criticize Me!

When words are many, sin is not absent,
but he who holds his tongue is wise.

Proverbs 10:19

Bonus Reading: 2 Corinthians 7:8–13

"Everyone stand in this line for ice skates!" Leslie called above the music of the skating rink. Leslie had been a children's worker for two years. She had gotten to know the second through fifth graders pretty well. Kelly, a fourth grader, had never been skating before. Leslie spent most of her time helping Kelly slip and slide along the ice.

After they removed their skates, Leslie remained seated while the children returned their rentals. Jake, the leader of the childrens ministries, came over and sat down next to her. "I noticed you spent a lot of time with Kelly today. Were you able to talk very much to the other kids?" he asked.

Leslie hesitated. "Yeah, I talked to Pete, Sandy, and Yvette. Why do you ask?"

Jake replied, "I overheard some kids say that you never pay any attention to them. That Kelly was your 'pet.'"

Leslie sat up straighter. "That's not true! I make it a point to say something to all the kids every meeting. Kelly just needed some extra help today." She grabbed her skates and stomped off toward the rental return, leaving Jake with his mouth open.

Outside the rink, Leslie and Jake said their good-byes to the children as the parents picked them up. After shutting the last car door, Jake tried again to talk with Leslie. "I didn't say that I agreed with the kids who thought Kelly was your pet. I just wanted you to know what they were saying. I know you love them all. We just want to 'avoid the appearance of evil.'"

Leslie sighed. "I guess I could have handed her off to one of the other workers or let her try it on her own against the rail. But she's so much fun to be with."

"You don't need to defend yourself. I might have done the same thing," Jake said.

Leslie kicked a pebble with her shoe and was silent for a moment. She looked up. "Sorry I yelled at you inside. I should have heard you out before getting angry and leaving."

Jake patted Leslie on the shoulder. "No problem. I'm just glad you didn't try to sock me."

"I would never . . . do . . . that!" Leslie grinned as she pounded his back.

When we feel defensive, we don't listen to what the other person is saying. Leslie's reaction cut off what Jake was trying to say. When others criticize us, we need to hear them out and think about what they are saying. We must realize that constructive criticism is meant for our good and not get angry with a person who is simply telling us the truth. We may not always agree with the opinion, but we need to honestly evaluate ourselves and decide what steps to take.

Lord, forgive me for overreacting to constructive criticism. Keep me calm and open to listen and to discern the truth. Give me a teachable spirit.

Surprise!

So Peter was kept in prison, but the church was earnestly praying to God for him. . . . But Peter kept on knocking, and when they opened the door and saw him, they were astonished.

Acts 12:5, 16

Bonus Reading: Acts 12:1–18

Daphne, a recent divorcée, joined a single moms support group. The women helped her deal with the emotional and spiritual turmoil she felt. Her ex-husband paid alimony and child support, but it wasn't enough to afford an apartment near the school where her children attended. With all the upheaval in their lives, she didn't want to upset the kids more by changing schools. Daphne couldn't work because of a medical condition, so she and her two kids barely scraped by.

The support group prayed for five weeks that Daphne would find an affordable apartment near school. In the meantime, Daphne found a place across town in a bad neighborhood. Loud music and shouting kept them up at night and Daphne had to fight traffic every morning to get her kids to school. Daphne almost couldn't bear the pressure.

One night, an hour before the support group met, Daphne's friend Gina called her. Her father's friend owned an apartment in the area Daphne wanted to live. Hearing her story, he was willing to rent it to her for half the usual amount! Ecstatic, Daphne called the man and made arrangements to see the place the next day.

Running in to the support group meeting late that evening, Daphne caught the last few words of a prayer. "Father, please help Daphne get an apartment closer to school. You know how much she needs it." Everyone looked up when Daphne exclaimed, "Girls, you'll never guess what happened!"

Are you surprised when God answers your prayer? Perhaps the early Christians didn't expect God to answer theirs so soon. They certainly didn't expect Peter to come knocking at their door in the middle of the night! Sometimes God answers in unusual ways.

Dear Lord, for some prayers I lack faith. Thank you for examples in the Bible of answered prayer. I know you care about me just as much as for the early Christians. Increase my faith in you.

Tradition versus Innovation

See to it that no one takes you captive through hollow and deceptive philosophy, which depends on human tradition and the basic principles of this world rather than on Christ.

Colossians 2:8

Bonus Reading: 1 Peter 1:18–19

Francesca, Hank, and Warren of the worship committee sat in front of Hank's fireplace, toasting marshmallows as they discussed the upcoming December service agenda.

"We always do the same thing for watch night every year," Hank complained. "Church goals—how they were fulfilled this year, how not; new goals for next year. Testimony time that gets wasted because no one stands up. A "B" movie. Refreshments at 10:30 and then most people leave to go to a really fun party. Hardly anyone's left at midnight to ring in the New Year."

Francesca nodded her head. "Why don't we do something different this time? We can make it fun so people will want to stay for the whole thing."

Warren held up one hand and counted with his fingers. "We have to ask ourselves: One, why do we have watch night? Two, what are we trying to accomplish? Three, what should we keep and what should we change?" He leaned back, eyeing his marshmallow. "Frankly, I don't want to chuck *all* the traditions our church has kept throughout the years. People will be thrown for a loop if everything is drastically different."

Hank took a flaming marshmallow out of the fireplace. He blew it out and said, "To answer your first question, I think watch night provides a safe and alcohol-free alternative to the world's version of the New Year's Eve celebration. It's mainly for Christians and their families. It gives the young people a place to go."

Francesca added, "It's also a time for the church family to unite spiritually and think about where we are as a body and where we want to go. Some people make New Year's resolutions. Why not the church?"

"Those are very valid points," Warren said. "Let's list elements of the past and possibilities for this year, and then see how they match up with our goals. From there, we can decide which traditions to keep as is, which to give a twist to, and where we can be totally innovative. Hopefully we can come up with a program that will be well-attended from beginning to end, that will glorify God, and will meet the needs of the people."

Innovation can be good, but traditions are also good if they serve a purpose. In the Bible, Jesus denounced the Pharisees for putting the traditions of men above God's Word. Some people take that as meaning *all* traditions are bad. We live in a fast-paced society that values innovation above convention. We must be careful to balance both sides and test them against the Bible.

Alpha and Omega, you know the beginning from the end. Help me to discern the value of traditions and innovations. My goal is to glorify you and if some of these do not, give me the courage to change them.

Filling Spaces on a Chart?

Then he said to his disciples, "The harvest is plentiful but the workers are few. Ask the Lord of the harvest, therefore, to send out workers into his harvest field."

Matthew 9:37–38

Bonus Reading: Matthew 9:35–38

Bridget was recruiting counselors for the middle and high school summer camp. She wanted to find men and women who could not only maintain order in the cabins, but also listen to teens and share with them from their hearts. Experience in counseling was a plus, but not a requirement. Bridget was planning to hold a one-day training session with all potential counselors.

Several months before camp, Bridget had made a chart listing whom she was planning to use in which age groups. As the week got closer, she began to worry about all the unfilled spaces on her chart. She wondered, *Should I allow anybody willing to become a counselor to do it, even if they don't meet all the requirements?*

Two weeks before camp, she received a more accurate number of campers to expect. Bridget was shocked when she realized she would need eight more counselors. "How am I going to find so many on such short notice?" she moaned aloud.

After discussing it with the pastor, Bridget made an announcement during service asking for potential counselors. A few people volunteered, ones Bridget would never have asked because she thought they weren't "counselor material." She held her training class and hoped it sufficiently prepared the new helpers.

On the first day of camp, Bridget had enough counselors for one or two per cabin—they usually had two or three. They made it through the week, however, and God blessed despite the circumstances. Bridget, however, felt disappointed in herself.

When we recruit volunteers, we are doing more than just filling spaces on a chart—we are helping people find a meaningful place of service in God's church. As much as possible, we should find people who have a heart and a passion for the ministry in mind. We should start early enough with a recruitment and training strategy that will enable us to find and equip qualified personnel in a timely manner. Most of all we need to ask God for wisdom and discernment in choosing the right helpers.

Wonderful Counselor, help me to find volunteers who have a passion for the ministry. Show me where to look and bring them across my path. Give me the resources to train them to serve you in this area.

I Want to Be like You

When the men of that place asked him about his wife, he said,
"She is my sister," because he was afraid to say, "She is my wife."
He thought, "The men of this place might kill me on account of
Rebekah, because she is beautiful."

Genesis 26:7

Bonus Reading: Genesis 12:10–20; 26:7–10

"Step right up and test your skill! Knock down all three bottles and
win a prize!" Todd shouted to the carnival goers.

"I'll try, Dad!" said seven-year-old Andre, running up to the
booth. He turned back to his mom and asked, "Would you hold
my snow cone, please?"

Liza took the icy treat. "After this, Dad and I will switch places.
I'll man the booth and he'll take you around the carnival."

Andre gave his dad a ticket and aimed a beanbag at a set of three
bottles, one placed on top of two. He threw with all his might. "Got
it! I win!" he shouted.

"Congratulations, son!" Todd held out a box of prizes and Andre
chose a parachute man.

He put it in his pocket and took back the snow cone from his
mom. Liza stepped over the front of the booth.

"Mom, didn't you have fun playing the games with me?" Andre
asked.

"Of course I did, Andre. But Dad and I volunteered to take care of
the booth. We're helping the church raise money for a new roof."

"Remember last winter when the rain leaked into your Sunday
school room and got the crafts all wet?" Todd reminded Andre.

"Oh yeah, everybody was sad when that happened." Andre
paused and took another lick from his snow cone. He looked up
and said, "Mom, Dad, can I help too? I want the church to get a
new roof!"

"Of course you can!" Todd and Liza both smiled as Todd lifted Andre over the front of the booth.

"Step right up and test your skill! Knock down all three bottles with one beanbag! Win LOTS of prizes!" Andre shouted to the crowd.

Andre followed the good example of his parents and chose to volunteer in the booth instead of playing the carnival games. Parents' actions and attitudes can influence their children positively or negatively. In the Bible, Isaac committed the same sin as his father, Abraham, when he lied about his wife, saying she was his sister. While no one is perfect, we should strive to be a good model to others by giving freely of our time and talents. They will be encouraged to do likewise.

Dear God, help me to be a good example to my children and others in the area of volunteering. May my life encourage others to willingly give of themselves to you.

Let Others Help

For you know that we dealt with each of you as a father deals with his own children, encouraging, comforting and urging you to live lives worthy of God, who calls you into his kingdom and glory.

1 Thessalonians 2:11–12

Bonus Reading: 1 Thessalonians 2:6–12

"Anita, would you like me to help you arrange those flowers?" a teenager asked.

"Oh, no. I can do it myself. When I'm done you can place them on the tables," Anita smiled.

"Anita, can I lend a hand with the chicken?" a college girl offered.

"I can handle the chicken. Why don't you find Lynnette and see if she needs help with the salad?" she suggested.

Anita coordinated the Valentine's Day banquet for one hundred married and engaged couples. As a gifted chef and florist, she had assisted with various church events in the past, but was never in charge of an entire function. Now as an administrator, she oversaw a committee of three who supervised thirty volunteers in cooking, setting and cleaning up, serving, and planning the program itself. Most of the helpers were middle school to young career age, many of them children of the married couples.

Anita planned the menu and bought all the food and flowers herself. Although plenty of people volunteered their help, she insisted on cooking the main course and arranging the table centerpieces herself because she wanted everything to be "just right." As a result, many young people were standing around with nothing to do and the banquet began an hour late.

Although the meal tasted excellent and the flower arrangements looked exquisite, some couples were disappointed they couldn't stay for the whole event because they had to pick up their young children from baby-sitters. The senior citizens left early too. The cleanup crew didn't finish their jobs until past 11:00 P.M. Anita went home exhausted, grouchy, and angry with herself. She felt like a failure.

Anita needed to resist the temptation to "micromanage." When we put others in charge of smaller areas, we should be there to encourage, mentor, and love them, as Paul did for the Thessalonians—not to perform their jobs. It doesn't matter so much that the tasks don't get done exactly the way we would do them as long as they are fulfilled to the best of your helpers' abilities.

Guiding Father, give me the ability to lead with compassion, patience, and sensitivity. Thank you for all those that work with me to serve you. I trust you will enable them to accomplish the task.

Decisions, Decisions

Here is a trustworthy saying: If anyone sets his heart on being an overseer, he desires a noble task.

1 Timothy 3:1

Bonus Reading: 1 Timothy 3:1–13; Proverbs 18:13, 15, 17

"Wait up, Simon!" Jerel yelled as he jogged up to the Sunday school room door. Simon had just picked up his son and was about to leave. "I have something to ask you."

Simon unconsciously tensed. *This was it. The big question.* Simon smiled and reached out to shake Jerel's hand. "What can I do for you?"

Jerel took Simon's hand and said, "It's not what I can do for you, but what you can do for the Lord. I have some great news for you. You've been nominated for two positions."

Simon looked startled. "Two? I'm almost afraid to ask what they are."

"You've been nominated for deacon and Christian school board member. Would you be willing to run for either one of them?"

Simon's eyes widened. He thought maybe he would be nominated for one position, but two? And ones that carried the most responsibility. "I'll have to think about it. I only have time for one and besides, I'm only *allowed* to run for one, right?"

"Right. Take your time thinking and praying about it. If you want to know more about the positions, I'd be happy to fill you in. You can even talk to some of the present deacons and school board members. Gotta go now." Jerel raised his hand in a wave.

Simon faced a dilemma. Which one should he choose? He was certainly qualified for both ministry opportunities. A church member for twenty years, he had taught Sunday school, fulfilled the requirements listed in 1 Timothy, and loved the people. His three children had attended the Christian school since kindergarten, the oldest now in high school. He was active in the parents group and knew most of the teachers and staff.

Simon and his family prayed every day for God's guidance. He talked with several deacons and school board members about their duties. He floated some of his ideas by both groups. Both wanted him to join their group. He searched the Scriptures for passages on deacons and leadership in general. He talked with his pastor and then his best friend. They expressed their opinions but basically said he had to make his own decision.

Finally, Simon committed himself. He opted for the school board position and immediately experienced relief. God's peace assured him that he had made the right choice.

Are you struggling with choosing between two volunteer positions? Pray for wisdom and then talk to others involved in the areas. Seek the advice of mature Christians whose judgment you trust. Search the Bible for any passages related to decision making. God's peace will enfold you as you discover his will.

Father, choosing between two good things is so hard. I need your guidance and wisdom to make the best decision. May your peace fill me as I seek and find your will.

Develop Your Skill

Sing to him a new song;
play skillfully, and shout for joy.

Psalm 33:3

Bonus Reading: 1 Chronicles 15:22; 25:7

Marjorie played clarinet in the church orchestra. The conductor rejoiced when she joined the group because the orchestra lacked clarinetists. As the sole clarinetist, however, Marjorie was at a disadvantage. Whenever she made a mistake, it was more noticeable because there were no other clarinetists to cover for her. And she made many errors.

Marjorie felt like quitting one Sunday afternoon after service was over. As she put her instrument away in the music room, the conductor walked up to her.

"I notice you look a little sad, Marjorie," Paula began. "Is there anything you want to talk about?"

"I'm just no good at the clarinet," Marjorie blurted out. "I think I would do the orchestra a favor if I quit."

Paula put her arm around Marjorie. "That's not true. We would all miss you very much. If you want, I can spend some extra time with you going over your part."

"I don't know if that would help. I only took clarinet in school for one year."

"I can help you with your technique too. I used to take clarinet lessons myself," Paula said.

Marjorie's face brightened. "Would you? I really want to play better."

"Of course. I'm glad you have the desire to improve yourself. God wants us to do our best for him. And part of that is developing our skills."

"You're right. Thank you so much, Paula. I'm glad we had this talk," Marjorie said as she closed her instrument case.

No matter what level of talent we possess, we can always improve. God is glorified when we use our gifts skillfully. He does not expect us to be perfect but to pursue excellence, which may include working harder, taking a refresher class, or surrounding ourselves with others who are like-minded.

Excellent Lord, thank you for the level of skill you have helped me achieve. You want me to do the best with what I have, which includes taking opportunities to improve myself. May I seize those openings to become the best I can be.

Ding Dong

When he comes, he will convict the world of guilt in regard to sin
and righteousness and judgment.

John 16:8

Bonus Reading: Acts 16:19–24

Cherie and Austin walked up to the door and rang the bell. They
waited anxiously for a few moments before a woman opened it.
"Hello, my name is Cherie and this is Austin. We're from South
Hills Church not far from here . . ."

"Sorry, not interested," the woman interrupted and shut the
door.

The two turned away. Austin said, "That's okay. Paul and Silas
got worse treatment."

Cherie bit her lip. "That's the second 'no' this day."

"At least she opened the door," Austin said. He unlocked the car.
"Forget about it. Let's drive to the next address."

The two drove in silence. As they got out of the car, they could
hear a television blaring from the house in front of them. They
checked the address and knocked on the door. A man yelled from
behind the door, "Who is it?"

Austin cleared his throat and shouted, "My name's Austin and
we're here from South Hills Church on Tenth Street. I believe your
son visited our church last week."

The television cut off. The door opened and a tall man in a T-shirt
stood before them. "Well, come on in," he said, smiling.

Cherie and Austin glimpsed a little boy peeking at them from
behind his father and heard a dishwasher going in the kitchen. They
looked at each other, smiled, and walked in.

Some people will be more receptive to a visit from the church than
others. We must not take rejection personally. Jesus himself was rejected

countless times. Don't give up. Keep praying and let the Holy Spirit do his work in hearts.

Heavenly Father, sometimes I get discouraged when I try to share the Good News with others. But I have to remember it is the Holy Spirit who convicts of sin and draws people to himself, not me. I am only a messenger. Help me to be a faithful one, even when no one seems to be listening.

Committed to the Cause

Then the Spirit came upon Amasai, chief of the Thirty, and he said: "We are yours, O David! We are with you, O son of Jesse! Success, success to you, and success to those who help you, for your God will help you."

1 Chronicles 12:18

Bonus Reading: Philippians 2:1–4

"Step right up and enter here!" the ringmaster shouted. "Fun, fun for everyone!"

Vacation Bible School buzzed with activity. The gym was decorated in a circus theme. Several children new to the church had signed up for this event. Sheldon, dressed as the ringmaster today, had worked hard coordinating VBS preparation. His friend Lee walked around dressed as a clown, greeting each student. Later on, Lee would perform his slapstick routine.

Two new families walked in together. Lee strolled up behind one child and tapped her on the shoulder. The girl turned around and screamed. One of her companions turned and cried too. The parents quickly hugged their children.

"I wanna go home!" cried one.

"I'm not going in there," sobbed the other.

An older child said, "If they don't have to go, I'm not going."

His friend said, "If he's not going, I'm not going either."

One parent quickly explained. "The little ones are deathly afraid of clowns. We didn't know there would be any here. I'm sorry, but I don't think we could get them to stay." She turned to leave.

Sheldon quickly said, "Hold on, don't leave yet. Let me see what I can do about the clown." He motioned for Lee to follow him.

When they were alone, Sheldon said, "For the sake of these two new families, let's remove the clown getup. You can still greet students and do your routine without it."

Lee's face fell. "But I busted my tail learning to be a clown. I like being a clown!" He waved his arms. "It won't be the same without the costume and makeup. Nobody will laugh."

Sheldon put a hand on Lee's shoulder. "I know you put a lot of effort into this. But think about these four new kids. We don't want to let this opportunity slip away from us. They can be reached with the gospel. I'm sure you can think of a way to modify your routine."

Lee sighed. "Yes, you're right. These kids are more important."

Sheldon patted Lee on the back. "That's the spirit. I knew you would understand."

Lee realized the mission of VBS was more important than his own agenda. He committed himself to the cause of Christ and set aside his personal preferences. In the Bible, Amasai committed his loyalty to King David and thus to God. How committed are we to God when our own preferences run contrary to the mission?

Great Leader, I want to serve you with all my heart. I don't want to put personal interests above your interests. Help me to be committed to your cause.

Small but Valuable

Are you the one to build me a house to dwell in? . . . I will raise up
your offspring to succeed you . . . He is the one who will build a
house for my Name.

2 Samuel 7:5, 12–13

Bonus Reading: 2 Samuel 7:5–13

Paulette sat down to lunch with Maxine at a crowded diner. Maxine
asked, "How do you like your new church?"

"It's fine. The kids are adjusting. Travis and I are thinking of
becoming members," replied Paulette.

The waiter came by with menus. After ordering, Maxine asked,
"Are you finding any new ministries to join?"

"Not yet. We're still pretty new. But the other Sunday, the person
who usually passes out bulletins was sick, so someone handed me
a stack to fill in," Paulette replied.

"That doesn't seem too exciting. After all, you used to be in charge
of so many ministries at your old church."

"On the contrary, it was a great experience. I felt good just doing
something for God, even if it was only passing out bulletins," Paulette said.

The two women continued chatting as they ate their meal. Toward
the end Maxine remarked, "I guess you're eager to get back into the
thick of things at church."

"Not in the way you would expect. At my old church, I was
doing so many things. Travis, too. But at the new one, I'm a nobody.
People there don't have preconceived ideas about us. They don't
expect us to be running around doing this and that. I find my own
ways to serve. The other day I was waiting for my son to get out of
youth group. I saw an overflowing garbage can and emptied it into
a bigger one. I feel that act was just as valuable as any job I did at
my old church," Paulette said.

As they rose from the table Maxine conceded, "I guess all roles are important, no matter how small they are."

Paulette found fulfillment in doing a small task for God. Although she was capable of more, it wasn't God's timing that she use all her talents right away at the new church. David desired to build God a house and had the financial resources to do it, but God wanted David's son Solomon to build it instead. Like David, Paulette accepted the tasks God did give her to do and did them heartily for the Lord.

Precious Father, you know I desire to serve you. I am willing to do any task for you, large or small. May I look for opportunities to serve you wherever you place me.

One Person at a Time

All they asked was that we should continue to remember the poor, the very thing I was eager to do.

Galatians 2:10

Bonus Reading: Deuteronomy 24:10–15

"How can we show hospitality to those in need?" I asked my Bible study group.

The seven women sitting around the oval dining-room table took turns giving suggestions. I noticed my assistant, Dawn, shifting uncomfortably in her chair. "Are there any other thoughts?" I asked.

Dawn blurted out, "I don't feel any compassion for the homeless, the poor, or anyone else like that. I also don't see how one person like me can do anything to help their situation."

During the next awkward moment of silence, I too admitted to myself that I felt indifferent to the down-and-out. *Why should I help people who probably got into their messes through their own fault? Why don't they help themselves? The government has plenty of programs to help the needy. Why doesn't God do something?*

Shannon, who had attended for the first time in six months, finally spoke up. "We may not be able to help everyone, but we can help one person at a time. Just this past week I heard of a woman named Marva who needs a bed. She's a single mother with three children and can't afford to buy a bed. I have some emergency money saved up and I'm seriously considering giving it to her."

As Shannon continued to describe Marva's need, my eyes teared up as I pictured her family sleeping on the floor. I was equally impressed with Shannon's concern for a woman whom she had never met. All of a sudden, I had a thought. My face began to flush with excitement as I realized it was no coincidence that Shannon came to Bible study that particular morning. I interrupted Shannon midsentence. "Keep your money, Shannon. I have a bed!"

The week before, my husband and I bought a new king-sized bed and we weren't sure what to do with our old queen. It was propped up against the wall of our living room. I made arrangements with Shannon for her to pick up the mattress, box spring, bed frame, and linens the following week and deliver everything to Marva.

Only God knew that Marva needed a bed and the Bible study leader had one. She couldn't imagine feeling compassion for all the needy, but when she heard Marva's story, her heart went out to her. When God connected her to Marva through Shannon, the whole Bible study group learned firsthand that God does indeed help the poor through willing people like them—one person at a time.

Dear God, I don't want to keep giving excuses for not helping the poor. Open my eyes to opportunities for good works even if I can help only one person. If one woman can help another, gather together many like-minded people who as a group can come to the aid of multitudes.

An Overflowing Well

Then, leaving her water jar, the woman went back to the town and said to the people, "Come, see a man who told me everything I ever did. Could this be the Christ?"

John 4:28–29

Bonus Reading: John 4:4–42

Barbara volunteered in a nursing home near her house. Twice a week she visited the residents to read them their mail, play board games, and do small chores. Her favorite resident, Arleta, always looked forward to her visits. Barbara would help the ninety-year-old out of bed and into her wheelchair to take her to the recreation room for a game of Scrabble.

On the way to the rec room, Barbara greeted all the residents they passed by name and stopped to chat with many of them, pushing Arleta along. She paused to help one man pick up some magazines he had dropped. As she wheeled Arleta into the room, she saw several other senior citizens lounging on chairs or sofas, heads down or staring out into space. Some looked up with interest as Barbara wheeled Arleta to a square table where a Scrabble board had already been set up. Barbara walked over to Harold and assisted him off a couch. Harold took hold of his walker and made his way slowly toward the ladies. After she seated Harold across from Arleta, Barbara sat down herself.

"Are you going to beat me again, Arleta?" Barbara asked, smiling.

"Depends on what kind of tiles I draw," Arleta replied.

"Don't forget about me," Harold reminded.

The game lasted about an hour and a half. Barbara helped the other two pick tiles and place them on the racks. Arleta's arthritic hands trembled as she placed her last tiles on the board. "I win!" she cried.

"Not again!" Harold moaned.

Barbara smiled at both of them. She placed all the tiles back in the box and left the game on the table. "I'll just have to come back next time and challenge you both again."

As Barbara wheeled Arleta back to her room, Arleta said, "I can't thank you enough for spending part of your life here with us. I can tell you're always happy to do it. If I were in your shoes, I don't think I could come to a place like this and help people the way you do. What's your secret?"

"Well, it makes me happy to bring happiness to others. But my real strength comes from the Lord. I try to fill my life with him so his love can overflow to others."

"Your cup surely runs over!" Arleta grinned.

Do you ever feel like your well is dry? Do you give so much that you feel like you have nothing more to give? We need to take time to refill our spiritual wells. The Samaritan woman left her physical water pots because she was filled with living water from Jesus Christ. Her newfound faith overflowed to everyone in her city. Sometimes our wells dry out, especially if we've been Christians for a while. We need to keep that water overflowing by praying, studying God's Word, and worshiping him on a regular basis. It's impossible to overflow when you are half empty.

Giver of living water, overflow my well. Fill me with your spiritual power so I may accomplish your will in my life.

"Volunteer" Does Not Equal "Christian"

But when the kindness and love of God our Savior appeared, he saved us, not because of righteous things we had done, but because of his mercy.

Titus 3:4–5

Bonus Reading: Titus 3:4–8

Jerome had loved soccer ever since he was in middle school. When the church formed a soccer team, he jumped at the chance to play. After he graduated from high school, he volunteered to coach the soccer team.

On his way home from practice one night, a car hit Jerome's on the freeway. He suffered a concussion and a broken leg. The pastor went to visit him in the hospital. During their conversation, the pastor brought up the question of his salvation.

"You mean all the times I went to Sunday school and all the volunteer hours I put in coaching soccer don't count for anything?" Jerome asked incredulously.

"Those are very good deeds and they benefited a lot of people, but they won't earn you a place in heaven," the pastor replied.

"But I grew up in the church. How can I *not* be a Christian?"

"A relationship with Christ isn't something you inherit from your parents. It begins when you realize your sin and ask Jesus to save you and come into your life."

"Well, how do I do that?"

The pastor patiently explained how to become a Christian. Jerome bowed his head and prayed that night to ask Jesus to be his Savior.

No matter how much you volunteer your time to help others or how many good works you perform, none of that is going to get you to heaven. After you become a Christian, you will want to do good works, not to earn or keep your salvation, but simply to please God and show your thankfulness to him for saving you.

Dear God, I realize now that I'm not really saved. I have been depending on the good things I do to earn a place in heaven. I know I'm a sinner and believe Jesus Christ came to earth to pay the penalty for my sin. Today I want to ask your Son Jesus to come into my life and I trust him to save me. Thank you for helping me realize my true condition.

Speak the Truth in Love

Speaking the truth in love, we will in all things grow up into him who is the Head, that is, Christ.

Ephesians 4:15

Bonus Reading: Proverbs 25:11; Matthew 7:4–5

The Easter drama ended with the scene of Christ ascending back to heaven in the clouds. The audience clapped wildly as the curtain fell. The hundreds of volunteers heaved a sigh of relief, praised God, and congratulated each other on a job well done.

One month later, the drama committee met to evaluate the program and begin planning for the following year. The director, producer, audiovisual supervisor, backstage manager, and musical director sat around a coffee table at the director's home.

The director began. "I want to thank you all for taking the time to meet together today. Each one of you put in a lot of work to make the Easter drama a success. Today we want to evaluate what was successful and also where we can improve. Feel free to express your opinions in a constructive manner. First of all, what was your overall reaction to the program?"

"I thought it was quite moving," the producer commented. "As I scanned the audience, I could tell they identified with the characters and understood the message. I talked to one visitor and she said it made her think about her own relationship to Christ." He took a sip of coffee. "That's what it's all about."

The others nodded in agreement. The director asked, "Are there any specific areas that seemed to work out well?"

The AV supervisor spoke up. "Once we ironed out that problem with the headsets, the AV and backstage could communicate really clearly with each other."

"And I could talk to everyone too," the director laughed. He put down his cup. "How about any unresolved problems?"

The committee members looked down at their coffee. The backstage manager took another sip of his drink. Finally the musical director spoke up. "On the night of the performance, there was still some confusion over when the choir was to sing a cappella and when the orchestra was to accompany. I think we needed to come to a decision earlier and stick with it."

The director leaned forward with his elbows on his knees. "You're right. I'm sorry I vacillated on that. I'll have to keep that in mind for next year."

The meeting continued and ended with suggestions for the following year. Everyone felt much was accomplished and left ready to tackle another program.

Does the above scenario seem too idyllic? Do your evaluation meetings end with hurt feelings, bitterness, and anger? Look up some biblical principles on criticism before confronting others or listening to others critique you. You may save yourselves from much stress, anxiety, and depression.

Loving God, I have to confront someone with a truth that may hurt. Help me to do it with compassion and help that person to receive it with a humble spirit.

Stay True to God

[Moses] said to Aaron, "What did these people do to you, that you led them into such great sin?"

Exodus 32:21

Bonus Reading: Exodus 32:21–24

Masato yelped as Shimon flicked a towel at him. "Hey, man, you got soap on my clothes. Aren't we supposed to be putting it on the cars?" Masato laughed as he threw a sponge back at Shimon.

Claude picked up a water hose. "Let me rinse you off," he said with a wicked grin.

"Okay, guys, get back to work," Pastor Juan said as he led another group of teenagers to a nearby car. "We've got ten vehicles lined up for you in the driveway. You can play later."

"Yes, sir!" Shimon said as he gave a mock salute.

Masato returned to scrubbing the tires of the SUV in front of him. Every year the youth groups of the church got together for a community car wash. Even before all the cars left, the teens managed to get in more than a few water fights.

"Why are you spending so much time on the tires, Masato? You heard Pastor Juan. We have ten more cars to go," Claude said.

"There's a lot of crud on them. Must have gone through the mud," Masato replied.

"Why bother? These people are getting their cars washed for free. They don't have to be absolutely spotless," Shimon said. "C'mon Claude, let's get to the next car."

"You're gonna miss the water fight if you don't hurry," Claude said over his shoulder as he and Shimon ran to a waiting minivan.

Masato shrugged his shoulders and returned to the tires. As he wiped off the third tire, he thought to himself, *I'm not going to let them bother me. I want to be a good testimony to whoever owns this car. I want to leave them with a good impression of the church. This is more important than a water fight.*

Masato smiled at the sparkling clean SUV. "This one's done, Pastor Juan!" he shouted as he picked up his bucket of soap water.

Masato did what he felt was right instead of giving in to the "herd mentality." He stayed true to his belief that the quality of his workmanship reflected his Christian testimony. Unlike Aaron in the Bible, Masato did not give in to the wishes of his peers.

> *Holy One, may I stay true to you even if others don't. Help me to do my best at whatever task you give me.*

Who Deserves the Credit?

Let him who boasts boast in the Lord.

2 Corinthians 10:17

Bonus Reading: Esther 2:22

Juanita and Claire handle publicity for various church functions and are both gifted artists. For the Family Celebration Dinner, the coordinator told them the theme and together the two women came up with a color scheme, a logo, and the font styles that would be used for all the publicity materials. For this event, they decided that Juanita would design the posters, written program, bulletin inserts, tickets, and invitations, and Claire would print them and make sure they got to the right people to distribute.

Several people commented that they liked the publicity materials, especially the posters. Whenever they complimented Claire, she would immediately tell them Juanita designed them. Whenever Juanita was commended, she would say that both she and Claire came up with the idea for the design together. On the program acknowledgments, Juanita put both their names under "Publicity."

At the end of the dinner, the emcee thanked everyone who helped with various aspects of the gala. He mistakenly announced that Claire designed the program and other materials. Claire couldn't correct him as she was sitting far away, but she did tell those sitting with her of Juanita's contribution. Juanita, at another table, outwardly smiled, but inside she was seething. *I spent hours at my drawing board and computer designing those things. Why did he give Claire credit and not me?*

After closing prayer, Juanita strode out the doors without speaking to anyone. Claire watched helplessly as there was no way she could run up and catch her. She just hoped Juanita would cool down before the next time they saw each other.

Despite her outward show of humility, Juanita cared very much that she got credit for her work. How do we react when someone else gets acknowledged, but we don't? Let's try to remember today's verse. If we have anything to boast about, it is the Lord's doing.

Lord, forgive me for being overly concerned with getting credit for my work. I thank you for the areas where you have gifted me. I must never take the credit for abilities you gave me. May my efforts truly glorify you and not me.

Bring All Your Gifts to the Team

And let us consider how we may spur one another on toward love and good deeds.

Hebrews 10:24

Bonus Reading: Exodus 36:1–3

The Christmas program rehearsal begins with the opening number. Herb ambles onstage with seven other carolers, stops in front of a door, sings "Joy to the World" and ambles off. His part is over. Or is it?

Herb chats backstage with his fellow carolers. "Hal, you're having back problems? I know a great chiropractor. Let me give you his number."

Herb notices the college kids painting scenery. "You guys are doing a good job. Do you need any help? I used to paint houses for a living."

Herb sees his friend who recently lost his spouse to cancer. "I know exactly how you feel, Paul. When my wife lost her battle with cancer, I couldn't stop thinking about her. If you ever want to talk, I'm here for you."

Herb has been to several rehearsals and knows exactly what to do on stage. He could think to himself, *I don't need to come to another practice. As long as I know my part, they don't really need me there.*

But Herb has a different attitude. When he comes to rehearsal, not only does he bring his singing ability, he brings all his knowledge, talents, and spiritual gifts with him. Herb uses his personal experience to help Hal with his back. As a retired house painter, he is willing to lend his expertise to the young people. He uses his gift of encouragement to help Paul with his grief.

Herb doesn't get bored practicing the same part over and over again. Singing is only part of his ministry. He sees rehearsal as a time for fellowship and encouraging his fellow cast and crew. He uses his "down time" to "build up" his brothers and sisters in Christ.

Do you limit yourself to one role and one role only at church? You are more than just a carpenter, cook, or choir member. You are a minister to your brothers and sisters in Christ. You affect each life you come in contact with. Will you use all your gifts for God?

Giver of all gifts, I thank you for my talents and spiritual gifts. May I willingly use them to glorify you and edify my fellow Christians.

Perfectionism versus Excellence

Not that I have already obtained all this, or have already been made perfect, but I press on to take hold of that for which Christ Jesus took hold of me.

Philippians 3:12

Bonus Reading: Matthew 25:14–30

"Let's try that last number one more time before calling it a night. This is our final rehearsal before the worship service tomorrow morning," Riga announced.

The troupe filed onto the auditorium stage and took their places. They began the interpretive dance number. Terri pirouetted to the right, but took too many steps and ran into another girl. They recovered and continued the program. Terri executed her solo perfectly. At the end, however, the eight high school girls were supposed to form a circle, but Terri was slightly out of position.

"Please let us do that number again, Riga. I know I can get it right," Terri pleaded from the stage. "People always remember the end."

"There's no more time. You'll do fine tomorrow," Riga assured.

"But I know I can do better," Terri insisted.

Riga walked up to the stage. She motioned for Terri to sit down on the edge. Riga sat down next to her. "Terri, you are an excellent dancer. But God doesn't expect you to be perfect. You do the best you can with the time and talent that you have. God will still be glorified when you try your best, even if you make mistakes."

"All right," Terri reluctantly agreed. "But we better pray hard tonight."

God wants us to strive for excellence in all that we do, but he understands we are not perfect. God alone is perfect. We must not set unrealistic goals for others or ourselves. We need to see ourselves as God sees us, sinners saved by grace with our own unique qualities. God has given to each of us certain talents and he will be pleased when we use them for him.

Spotless Savior, thank you for making me the way you did. Thank you for the talents that you have given to me. Help me to use them for your glory. Forgive me if I have been trying to be a perfectionist. Help me, though, to do my best for you.

I Can't Always Be There

"Men of Galilee," they said, "why do you stand here looking into the sky? This same Jesus, who has been taken from you into heaven, will come back in the same way you have seen him go into heaven."

Acts 1:11

Bonus Reading: Acts 1:7–11

Ramon held a cell phone to his ear as he sped toward the airport. "Lars, my father fell and broke his hip. I'm taking the next flight out to see him. I'm afraid I can't make the Father-Son Camping Trip this weekend."

"So sorry to hear about your dad. Don't worry about the trip. Niles and I can take care of it. We can't disappoint forty guys, can we?" Lars said.

"You're a pal, Lars. I've got camping and sports equipment in the garage. But you'll have to buy all the food. I left a list with my wife," Ramon said as he turned into the airport.

"Piece of cake. It's about time you let someone else be in charge. After all, you've been doing it for five years."

"I think you're ready for it. You helped last year, so you know what to do." Ramon pulled into a parking space. "Let me know how everything turns out. I should be back sometime next week." He hung up, pulled a small suitcase from the backseat, and dashed into the terminal.

A week later, Ramon returned. As he drove out of the airport he phoned Lars. After telling Lars his father was recovering quickly, he asked, "How'd everything go with the camping trip?"

"It went pretty well. We had fun despite the fact that it rained the second night and I didn't have a backup plan. But Niles was really good at improvising. We sure missed you, though."

"The important thing is that everyone still had a good time," Ramon said.

"Yes, they did. Nothing beats a crisis for pulling people together. I think the fathers and sons really bonded this weekend," Lars said.

The camping trip was a success despite the leader not being able to attend. Because Ramon had trained his helpers well and left them resources, his team was able to function without him. Even if it wasn't as organized, the main purpose of bonding and fellowship was accomplished. When Jesus left the apostles, he gave them the Holy Spirit to guide them and to be their Source of comfort and power. They had sat under Christ's teaching for three years and after he left had to utilize what they had learned.

Dear God, there are times when I can't always be there for my teammates. Help them to keep going without me and accomplish your will.

I'm the Best

Let him who boasts boast about this:
  that he understands and knows me,
that I am the Lord, who exercises kindness,
  justice and righteousness on earth,
for in these I delight.

Jeremiah 9:24

Bonus Reading: 2 Corinthians 12:9

Antoinette sauntered into the choir room twenty minutes late. With head held high she walked right past the childrens choir director and took her seat in the girls section. As Mavis led the group, she eyed Antoinette disappointedly. When Antoinette finally settled in her chair, the song was over.

"Let's start again from the top," Mavis instructed.

As the choir sang, Antoinette's voice rang out clear and beautiful. Mavis admitted to herself the song sounded better with Antoinette's strong voice. At the end of the first verse, the music indicated a solo part.

Mavis said, "Instead of a solo, we're going to have all the girls sing this part."

Antoinette raised her hand. "Miss Mavis, I think I should sing the solo."

The other children looked at each other. Some of the boys snickered. Mavis said, "I think it would be better if all the girls sang it."

"But I'm the best singer," Antoinette said matter-of-factly.

More snickers. Mavis glared at them. She turned to Antoinette. "Let's talk after practice."

After the other children left the room, Mavis sat down next to Antoinette. "Antoinette," she began, "I care about you very much. You are a sweet girl and God has given you a very beautiful voice." Antoinette smiled. "But the reason I'm not having you do the solo is because I don't want you to—how shall I say this—get a big head over it."

Antoinette stopped smiling and shifted uncomfortably in her seat. Mavis continued. "Let me show you something in the Bible." She turned to 2 Corinthians 10:17–18. "Can you read these two verses?"

Antoinette peered at the Bible. "Let him who boasts boast in the Lord. For it is not the one who commends himself who is approved, but the one whom the Lord commends." She looked up. "What does this mean?"

"It means we shouldn't seek our own praise, but God's praise. If we are talented in a certain area, thank God for that. But we don't want to think we are better than everyone else. Does that make sense?"

Antoinette nodded. "I guess I've been a little prideful, huh?"

Mavis patted Antoinette on the shoulder. "I think you understand."

Adults may exhibit an attitude of superiority in more subtle ways. Being habitually late, aloof, unprepared, or resistant to teaching may be signs of pride. We must constantly guard ourselves against thinking more highly of ourselves than we ought.

Most High, I must confess I don't always have a humble attitude. Maybe that's why I fall flat on my face sometimes. You are the reason I can accomplish anything.

Such a Time as This

For if you remain silent at this time, relief and deliverance for the
Jews will arise from another place . . . And who knows but that you
have come to royal position for such a time as this?

Esther 4:14

Bonus Reading: Esther 3:1–4:14

Sondra's stomach tightened. As she walked the corridor to Pastor
Graves's office, she rehearsed silently what she would say. *I think
your plan to expand the church ministries is good. I support your
ideas, but as they are now, I think the womens ministries are being
overlooked. We would like to start a support group for women suffering
from depression.*

Sondra had been a church member for twenty years and had
served in just about every area open to her. She didn't want to sound
like a know-it-all or a complainer, but she had to tell him what she
thought. She had not talked to anyone about her feelings, fearing
she would be labeled as a troublemaker.

As Sondra sat waiting outside Pastor Graves's office, she remembered Queen Esther. The Jews were condemned to die. Esther was
afraid to speak to the king on their behalf because she could be
killed if she came into his presence without being called. Only if
the king held out his golden scepter to her would she be allowed to
live. Sondra took a deep breath of determination as she remembered
the outcome. Esther did find favor with the king and did save the
Jews from annihilation.

Sondra jumped when Pastor Graves opened his door. "Come in,
Sondra. What can I do for you today?"

Sondra breathed a silent prayer. *Lord, you've placed me here for
such a time as this. Show me what to say.* She picked up her purse
and walked through the open door.

If you need to accomplish a difficult task, don't be afraid to act. Ask for courage and God's direction to do what is very hard for you. Like Esther, you may have been placed in your position "for such a time as this."

O Lord, I am so scared. I want to do the right thing, but it is really hard. Give me courage like Esther and help me do what needs to be done in a way pleasing to you.

Passing the Torch

Likewise, teach the older women to be reverent in the way they live
. . . to teach what is good. Then they can train the younger women
. . . so that no one will malign the word of God.

Titus 2:3–5

Bonus Reading: 2 Kings 2:1–14

Andy enjoyed preparing the graphics and layout of the church newsletter. However, his other church duties kept growing and he knew
he didn't have time to put forth his best effort in all of them. After
much prayer and reflection, he felt he should drop the newsletter,
but did not know of anyone who could take his place.

After several weeks of asking around, Andy found out about
Cole. Cole had just graduated from college and had flown back
into town a few days earlier. Since he had majored in computer
graphics and was very artistic, Cole seemed the ideal person to take
Andy's place.

When Andy finally met Cole and spoke with him about helping
with the newsletter, Cole became very excited. "That's right up my
alley," he exclaimed. "I know I can be an asset to the newsletter."

Andy began meeting with Cole once a week. In the process, they
spent a lot of time together. Not only did Andy teach the young
man how to produce the newsletter, he became a valuable friend
and mentor to him.

Training others to eventually replace you ensures the life of a ministry
and increases your productivity for God. Before Elijah left this earth, he
had trained Elisha to take his place. Mentoring someone takes time,
patience, and energy, but in the long run, pays off. You will feel less
pressured to stay with a ministry when God is leading you away from it
if you have someone prepared to fill your shoes.

Mighty Mentor, thank you for the many ministry opportunities you have provided me. Now is the time to pass the torch to someone else in one area so I can concentrate more fully in another. Help me find the right person to take my place.

Sweating the Small Stuff

We went into the land to which you sent us, and it does flow with milk and honey! Here is its fruit. But the people who live there are powerful, and the cities are fortified and very large. We even saw descendants of Anak there.

Numbers 13:27–28

Bonus Reading: Numbers 13:25–33

Lloyd and Madeline cruised the warehouse store aisles picking out items for the church's Thanksgiving food baskets. Their two carts brimmed over with frozen turkeys, stuffing mix, rolls, fresh vegetables, canned cranberry sauce, and jarred gravy. Lloyd held a calculator in one hand as he pushed one cart with the other.

"We've reached the limit of our budget. Let's get in line to pay for all this stuff," Lloyd said.

On their way to the front of the store, they passed an aisle filled with wicker baskets and wrapping supplies. "Lloyd, look! Those baskets would be perfect to put all the food in. We can buy some ribbon too and make beautiful bows," Madeline exclaimed.

Lloyd held up his calculator. "We don't have any more money for extras. There are lots of empty boxes in the front of the store. We can just use those."

"But, Lloyd, they'll look so pretty in the baskets with the bows. Maybe we can put back the gravy and the cranberry sauce and even the rolls. Some people make their own gravy or don't like cranberry sauce or rolls."

"I think the folks we're giving this stuff to would appreciate the food more than the fluff," Lloyd said, tapping his foot. "They're hungry, remember?"

"All right. You win. But if we get more money, I'm coming back," Madeline said.

Madeline was more concerned with the way the food was presented than the quantity of food given. Although it's nice to receive a beautifully wrapped gift, in this case what was inside was probably more important to the recipients. Madeline was concerned about a small matter rather than looking at the big picture of feeding hungry people. The ten spies who came back to the Israelites reported that the land was fruitful, but focused on the powerful enemies they would have to deal with and not on how powerful their God was to overcome them.

God, sometimes I am worried about all the little details I need to figure out rather than focusing on the big picture. Help me not to sweat the small stuff and keep my focus on you.

No One Will Know

In everything set them an example by doing what is good. In your teaching show integrity, seriousness and soundness of speech that cannot be condemned, so that those who oppose you may be ashamed because they have nothing bad to say about us.

Titus 2:7–8

Bonus Reading: Acts 6:1–7

Cassidy and Delicia sang in a small womens ensemble at church. The group was preparing to sing for Mother's Day and needed to find an appropriate song. They didn't want to sing something they used before and could not find anything they liked that was specifically for Mother's Day.

As they sat around the grand piano at Delicia's home. Cassidy suggested, "Why don't we use a song we know, but change the words to fit the occasion? That way, we'll already know the parts and will just have to memorize new words."

Delicia asked, "Don't we have to get permission from the composer or publishing house to make those changes and perform the song in public?"

The others looked at each other and shrugged their shoulders. Cassidy said, "We're such a small church, no one's going to know. It's not like the police are going to come and arrest us."

"I would still feel better if we got their permission," Delicia said. "Tell you what, I'll write a letter and you write the lyrics, then we'll fax them both to the publisher."

"Okay, I guess you're right," Cassidy said. The others nodded in agreement. "We should try to do what's right, even if we could get away with doing wrong."

The womens ensemble decided to do what is proper by writing to the publisher and thus maintaining a good testimony. The early church chose seven men of good reputation, filled with the Holy Spirit and with wisdom to wait on the widows' tables. As Christians and as artists we should never do anything that would make someone question our integrity.

Sinless Savior, help me to maintain a good testimony for you, even when it is inconvenient or I think no one is watching. You are always watching and I desire to please you in everything I do.

Star Players

If one part suffers, every part suffers with it; if one part is honored, every part rejoices with it.

1 Corinthians 12:26

Bonus Reading: 1 Thessalonians 5:11

The chatter of the cast and crew greeted Donavan as he stepped backstage to congratulate Chuck, his old college roommate and director of the Christmas program. Donavan remarked, "Those women who played the two competing innkeepers sure had me believing they really hated each other. They were at each other's throats." He whispered, "Are they like that in real life?"

Chuck laughed. "Not at all. They're good friends. They've been in lots of plays together. They always encourage each other before coming out on stage."

Donavan raised an eyebrow. "With talent like that I'm surprised they don't get jealous of each other."

Chuck said, "I can't see into their hearts, but from what I can tell, they are genuinely happy for the other when one gets a good part."

"In the 'real' world, that's very rare. People with overlapping talents tend to see each other as threats," Donavan noted.

Chuck nodded in understanding. "I'm not saying that that never happens here, but we think of each other as being on the same team. We don't compete with each other. When one does well, we are all happy for her."

"And when one does poorly?"

"We don't gloat, but all try to console her."

"If that's really true, maybe there is something to your Christianity," Donavan conceded as they headed toward the cast party.

Do you have team spirit in your ministry? If so, you are a positive testimony to the world of Jesus Christ's love and power. Praise God for your talents and the talents of your teammates. Keep encouraging each other to give God your finest.

Dear God, thank you for my natural talents and the opportunities to hone and use them for you. Thank you for giving others in my ministry their abilities. Help us to never become jealous of each other or have a competitive spirit. Use our strengths and weaknesses together to glorify your name.

Take Ownership

So the warden put Joseph in charge of all those held in the prison, and he was made responsible for all that was done there.

Genesis 39:22

Bonus Reading: Genesis 39:20–23; 41:33–40

As Dionne and Marla took their weekly treadmill walk at the gym, Dionne said flatly, "Our son Will is talking about leaving the church."

"How can he mean that?" Marla exclaimed. "He's grown up in the church, attended all the youth groups. He was even baptized last year."

"He says when he starts college next year, he's going to look for another church. I asked him what the problem was and he says he doesn't feel like this is 'his' church, but it's his parents' church," Dionne tried to explain as she slowed down the treadmill. "He says it belongs to the grown-ups and not the kids. He says it reflects our way of doing things and not the young people's." Dionne held onto the rails. "He wants out."

"Come to think of it, I've heard other parents say similar things about their kids. I would say half the kids leave our church when they graduate from high school." Marla stopped her machine. "I don't begrudge them looking for opportunities to serve God elsewhere, but it's a shame more don't stay at our church to serve the Lord." She reached for her towel.

Dionne got off her treadmill. "How can we encourage our children to 'take ownership' of the church?" she asked. "What will make it feel like 'their' church?"

The two women headed over to the water fountain. Marla said, "I try to include my kids in my ministries, like in preparing arts and crafts materials. When Sasha got too old to attend Vacation Bible School, I encouraged her to help out. She loved being on 'the other end' of VBS. It made her feel important."

Dionne splashed water on her face. "I hear Pastor Bob is looking for helpers for the middle school club. College-aged adults would be great role models for them. I wonder if Will might consider volunteering for that instead of leaving?"

"He might." Marla took a few sips from the fountain. "The other day Sasha told me about an idea she had for a youth group meeting. When she talked to Pastor Bob about it, he told her to get her thoughts down on paper and write a proposal. He didn't shoot her down and say it was a bad idea. He put the responsibility back on her to focus her idea and make it workable."

"That would be a great test of her ingenuity and perseverance," Dionne commented. "I heard that the college group at another church made up their own VBS curriculum and used it last summer for the elementary school children. One of the college guys gave a testimony about how 'cool' it was to see how something he created affected other people's lives. I sure hope our church can do something like that."

"Perhaps we can suggest it to Pastor Bob. I'm sure he's aware of the problem, but maybe he needs to know the parents are willing to put some effort into keeping their children here," Marla said as they walked toward the locker room.

When Joseph proved himself to be faithful in small tasks, he was given larger tasks until he became second in command over Egypt. When our children help do small things around the church, it prepares them for volunteer positions in adulthood. Encourage your children to take ownership of their church. When they become adults, they may feel more inclined to stay.

Our Father, we thank you for the children and young people of our church. Thank you for the energy and enthusiasm they lend to church ministries. Please keep them under your care as they grow to maturity. Help them to see themselves as loved and useful to you and their church.

What's the Real Reason?

Should you then seek great things for yourself? Seek them not.

Jeremiah 45:5

Bonus Reading: Acts 8:17–24

Ward donated his time-share in Hawaii to the Christian school auction. One week at a Maui resort right next to the beach! News of this exotic vacation item spread quickly throughout the campus. When Ward picked up his kids after school, all the parents asked him about his donation.

"What's the name of the resort? Does it have a big pool?" one father asked.

"You're willing to give up your week in paradise for the school? That's very noble of you!" said a mother.

"You must really believe in the school to donate something like that!" another parent commented.

Ward grinned and answered all their questions willingly. He even passed around pictures of his last vacation there.

When Camille, the auction coordinator, called him and asked the value of his time-share, Ward mentioned an exorbitant amount. "I can't print that in the program, Ward," she said. "It's not realistic."

"I'm adding in sentimental value. What's wrong with that?"

"It wouldn't be exactly truthful. Then I would have to set the opening bid higher and no one will be able to afford it. It may not sell at all."

"You can start the bidding at one dollar," Ward said. "Then lots of people will bid."

"You've got to be kidding! If we start that low, the highest bidder will stop at half of what it's worth and the school won't make much money. Let's be reasonable here."

"My terms or I withdraw my item."

The two dickered for a while and finally reached a compromise. On the night of the auction, the low opening bid and high retail value listed fed a bidding frenzy. The time-share was the most popular item, but in the end did not draw in the most money for the school. But Ward got what he wanted.

On the surface, Ward desired to help the school by donating his time-share, but in reality, he just craved attention. In the Bible, Simon had selfish reasons when he offered to pay the apostles money for the power to impart the Holy Spirit to others. We must examine our own motives whenever we serve God to make sure they are pure.

Searcher of hearts, sometimes when I serve you, I do have other reasons than simply because I love you. Some of these reasons are selfish. Forgive me and help me serve with a pure heart.

Time for Self

Then, because so many people were coming and going that they did not even have a chance to eat, he said to them, "Come with me by yourselves to a quiet place and get some rest."

Mark 6:31

Bonus Reading: Exodus 31:12–17

Cliff was exhausted. After working a full day at an accounting firm, he faced more financial tasks at home. As church treasurer, he took care of bookkeeping and all money matters. The church was planning to hire a full-time accountant, but until then, Cliff took care of everything from organizing people to counting offering to preparing financial statements for the church business meetings.

After dinner, Cliff played with his two children in the family room. Afterward, his wife, Darlene, hustled them off to wash up and get ready for bed. Cliff started toward his computer in the den to finish the monthly balance sheet for the deacons meeting. As he reached down to press the "on" button, he thought, *This can wait. I need to take some time for myself.*

He straightened up and walked out to the garage to his woodworking bench and began sanding the legs for his new desk. After an hour, he went back inside to his computer, refreshed and ready to tackle the balance sheet.

Meanwhile, Darlene cleaned up the kitchen. She also worked full-time and was tired from a long day. After putting the kids to bed, she sat down on the living room couch and put her legs up on the ottoman. She fingered the pages of her novel and instantly lost herself in the story.

Before retiring for the night, Cliff joined Darlene in the living room. They sat by the fireplace and watched the logs crackle. They discussed their days and chatted about the children and what was really important in life. They both relaxed and were ready for a good night's rest.

Sometimes our lives are so busy we need to schedule time for relaxation. Jesus knew the value of rest and encouraged his disciples to take care of themselves. Cliff and Darlene made time for themselves and each other. When we "recharge our batteries" we become more productive and ready to face the challenges of life.

Renewer of my soul, grant me the rest I desperately need. Help me make time for myself so I can serve you better.

Be Honest

Whoever can be trusted with very little can also be trusted with much, and whoever is dishonest with very little will also be dishonest with much.

Luke 16:10

Bonus Reading: Proverbs 16:11

"That'll be $16.00 for two adults and two children," Craig said as he counted out four tickets. The purchaser handed Craig a twenty dollar bill and Craig gave him four dollars change. "See you at the picnic!" Craig waved as the man and his family walked off.

Craig was in charge of selling tickets and buying food and supplies for the church picnic. He kept careful records of how much he collected each Sunday before the event. Everyone paid by cash and he kept the money at home in a safe place.

A few days before the picnic, Craig drove to the supermarket to buy the necessary items. After paying the cashier he still had forty dollars left over. As he was pushing the cart to his car, he thought, *I haven't told anyone yet how much I collected. With over three hundred tickets sold, who's going to count how many people are at the picnic? I can just throw away the extra tickets so no one will know exactly how many were sold. If anyone bothers to ask, I can just change a few numbers on my records.*

As Craig closed the trunk of his car, he rationalized, *I deserve to keep the extra money after all the work I've done. I've earned it.*

The day of the picnic, Craig sat under a tree with his friends, eating a hot dog, laughing at a joke someone just told. One of the others asked, "So Craig, how much money did you collect?"

Craig almost choked on his hot dog. After swallowing, he managed to say, "Enough to pay for everything."

"Did you have anything left over?" another friend asked.

Craig took a gulp of his soda. "Not much, just a little spare change." He wiped his brow. "Sure is hot today. Good day for a picnic."

The conversation took off in another direction. Craig finished the last of his meal and stood up to throw his plate away. He spied the picnic coordinator at the far end of the park. He reached into his pocket and felt where the forty dollars lay. He looked back at his friends. He looked at the beautiful lake next to the picnic grounds. He thought to himself, *I can't do it. I can't cheat the people I love and I can't steal from God.*

Craig walked determinedly toward the coordinator. He took the money out of his pocket and before she could say anything, he said, "Here's forty dollars left over from the ticket sales. I can turn in my records and receipts too. They're in the car."

The coordinator looked momentarily surprised. "Why, thank you, Craig. I'll turn this in to the church treasurer today. We'll have forty extra dollars to spend on next year's picnic. Maybe you could take my place and be in charge."

Craig laughed and turned away. His heart felt light as he ran over to join a volleyball game.

How often we are tempted to not give an object back that we "borrowed" from church because it is inconvenient, or because we "forgot," or because we think "No one is going to miss it." Perhaps you bought something for a church ministry and all of it was not used, so you kept the rest for yourself without asking if it was okay to do so. God rewards honesty even in small matters, especially with a guilt-free conscience.

Lord, help me to be honest, especially with church funds. Everything belongs to you — I am just a steward. May I be a faithful one.

Failing Graciously

> But he said to me, "My grace is sufficient for you, for my power is made perfect in weakness."
>
> 2 Corinthians 12:9

Bonus Reading: Joshua 7:3–13; 8:1

Angela, Elise, and Nick put together a special singing number combining members from two college-aged church clubs. Angela was the keyboardist, Nick the conductor, and Elise one of the ten singers. All the musicians attended the same college where they also held rehearsals. The clubs were joining for a meeting on Christian love and unity. The event would take place at Angela's church.

As an average pianist, Angela needed to practice really hard to make sure she didn't mess up. Nick worked diligently to help all the singers learn their parts, blend, and sound as one. Elise learned her part well and tried her best to maintain a sense of unity and cooperation among the group.

Seventy-five young people filled the church chapel. Their chatter died down as the singers stepped onto the platform. Angela placed her book onto the music holder of the keyboard. She creased the dog-ear at the bottom of the second page. Nick nodded for her to begin. The singers came in exactly as Nick motioned them to. Their voices filled the air with enthusiasm.

Turning the page, Angela's fingers slipped on the dog-ear. She managed to get to page three, but lagged one beat behind. She continued playing, but threw everyone off. Nick couldn't figure out how to get the singers and piano back together again. Elise realized Angela lagged behind, but was afraid to be the only one to correct herself.

The ensemble stopped singing, one person at a time. Needless to say, the special number disintegrated by the time Angela finished the song. Angela felt she had failed everyone—not just the singers, not just the audience, but God himself. After all, the group was supposed to symbolize unity and oneness. How could they do that if they couldn't even sing together?

After the meeting, Angela walked up to Nick and Elise. "I'm so sorry for messing everyone up."

Nick replied, "No, it was my fault as the conductor for not getting everyone back together."

Elise jumped in, "No, it was *my* fault for not following the keyboard. I knew what happened but didn't do anything."

Angela stared in amazement at the two of them. They were so apologetic and willing to take the blame for her mistake. She managed to say, "I guess next time I'll have someone else turn pages for me."

The ensemble participants actually met the goal of the meeting. Angela's weakness turned out to be the catalyst for an amazing show of Christian love. Instead of blaming her, the others tried to make her feel better by taking the blame themselves. The special number did not fail in God's eyes. Not only did the musicians learn from their mistakes, but also they demonstrated God's love to each other.

Unfailing Lord, thank you for using even my weaknesses to glorify your name. Thank you for the love of my fellow brothers and sisters in Christ. May I love others despite their faults.

Be Unconventional

There the angle of the LORD appeared to him in flames of fire from
within a bush. . . . So Moses thought, "I will go over and see this
strange sight—why the bush does not burn up."

Exodus 3:2–3

Bonus Reading: Exodus 3:1–5

As Misty stood sorting her mail, she spied a small envelope with
her address handwritten in cursive on the front. She gingerly loos-
ened the flap and pulled out a card that said, "You're Invited . . ."
Eagerly, she opened it and read, ". . . to a Progressive Dinner." As
she quickly scanned the contents she began to chuckle. *That Pastor
Dirk sure is creative.*

On the appointed night, Misty arrived at Pastor Dirk's home. He
greeted her at the door and ushered her to the family room where
seven other guests sat chatting. Pastor Dirk cleared his throat and
began. "Since we're all here now, I would like to welcome you to
our progressive Sunday school department heads training dinner.
While you're enjoying your appetizers," he pointed to a plate of
cheese and crackers, "I want you to ask each other, 'What do you
like about teaching Sunday school?'"

The guests smiled and began talking about their classes. After five
minutes, Pastor Dirk got everyone's attention and said, "Now we
will 'progress' to the breakfast nook where we will enjoy our salad.
At the same time, I will be going over some announcements that
will affect all your departments."

The guests chuckled and moved over to the breakfast nook where
Pastor Dirk's wife had set up eight salad plates. "Aren't you two going
to eat?" Misty asked.

"We'll eat our salad with the entrée," Pastor Dirk said with a
twinkle in his eye.

After he gave grace, Pastor Dirk made his announcements. "Feel
free to eat while I'm talking," he reminded them.

When everyone finished, they were ushered into the formal dining room. A portable television with built-in VCR sat at the end of the room. Meat loaf, mashed potatoes and gravy, and steamed mixed vegetables lined the center of the rectangular table, ready to be served family style. After everyone got their portions, Pastor Dirk turned on the television and VCR. The guests watched an instructional video discussing different learning styles—visual, auditory, tactile, and kinesthetic.

After dinner, everyone helped clear the table and then moved on to the living room for dessert and coffee. Misty remarked, "Now I understand why one little girl in my class just can't sit still and listen. She's not an auditory learner."

"I'm glad the video helped you understand your student better," Pastor Dirk said. He turned to address everyone. "While you enjoy your chocolate chip cookies, let's discuss how we can take what we've learned from the video and apply it to our own classrooms."

The evening came to a close and as the guests left, Pastor Dirk handed them notes from his announcements and the video. As Misty took her papers, she said, "I probably won't need the notes because this has been the most memorable and enjoyable Sunday school department heads meeting I've ever been to. I think I used all the learning styles tonight. I'm going to do something like this next time I have a primary department meeting."

Pastor Dirk's unusual teaching method aroused the interest and enthusiasm of his teachers. In a similar fashion, God caught Moses' attention when he appeared in a bush that kept burning. Sometimes we need to think of new ways to engage our learners whether they are our own children or others we minister to.

Dear God, you have made each person unique, especially in the way each learns best. Help me think of creative ways to teach others.

Quick Collect

Pay to Federal Bureau
of Prison

Attentin - Kevin L Howard

11923171.

Reference # 11923171 Howard

Code City F B O P

State D.C.

Senders Info
acct# 11923171 Howard
phone #
address

Scripture Index

191

Carol Lee Hall got hooked on volunteering as a junior high student and has since volunteered numerous hours in a variety of church and school activities. She is a freelance writer whose work has appeared in *Today's Christian Woman* and the San Jose *Mercury News*. Carol, her husband, and their daughter live in Fremont, California. To find out more about Carol, visit her web site: www.carolleehall.com.